# Cambridge Lower Secondary

# Complete English

Series Editor: Dean Roberts
Annabel Charles, Alan Jenkins,
Mark Pedroz, Tony Parkinson

Second Edition

**8**

# WORKBOOK

OXFORD
UNIVERSITY PRESS

# OXFORD
## UNIVERSITY PRESS

Great Clarendon Street, Oxford, OX2 6DP, United Kingdom

Oxford University Press is a department of the University of Oxford.

It furthers the University's objective of excellence in research, scholarship, and education by publishing worldwide. Oxford is a registered trade mark of Oxford University Press in the UK and in certain other countries

© Oxford University Press 2021

The moral rights of the author have been asserted

First published in 2021

British Library Cataloguing in Publication Data
Data available

978-1-38-201937-8

10 9 8 7 6 5 4

Paper used in the production of this book is a natural, recyclable product made from wood grown in sustainable forests.

The manufacturing process conforms to the environmental regulations of the country of origin.

Printed in China by Shanghai Offset Printing Products Ltd

## Acknowledgements

**Cover**: beastfromeast/Getty Images

**Artworks**: Integra

**Photos**: p61: 'Railhead' by Philip Reeve (OUP, 2016). Reproduced with permission of the Licensor through PLSclear

The publisher would like to thank the following for permissions to use copyright material:

**Carl Sandburg**: Excerpt from "Jazz Fantasia" from THE COMPLETE POEMS OF CARL SANDBURG, Revised and Expanded Edition. Copyrighi @ '1969, 1970 by Liiian Steichen Sandburg, Tustee. Reprinted by permission of Houghton Mifflin Harcourt Publishing Company. All rights reserved.

**Debjani Chatterjee**: 'Hungry Ghost' was published in 'A Little Bridge' by Debjani Chatterjee et al (Pennie Pens, Hebden Bridge, 1997). Used by permission from the author.

**Malorie Blackman**: 'Thief' by Malorie Blackman. Copyright © Malorie Blackman. Reproduced by permission of A.M. Heath & Co Ltd.

**Berlie Doherty**: 'Street Child' (HarperCollins, 2009), copyright © Berlie Doherty 1993, reproduced by permission of David Higham Associates.

Every effort has been made to contact copyright holders of material reproduced in this book. Any omissions will be rectified in subsequent printings if notice is given to the publisher.

This Workbook refers to the Cambridge Lower Secondary English (0861) Syllabus published by Cambridge Assessment International Education.

This work has been developed independently from and is not endorsed by or otherwise connected with Cambridge Assessment International Education.

This Workbook refers to the Cambridge Lower Secondary English (0861) Syllabus published by Cambridge Assessment International Education.

This work has been developed independently from and is not endorsed by or otherwise connected with Cambridge Assessment International Education.

# Table of contents

# Foodies' delight

## My life on a plate – food interviews

If possible, interview a family member, neighbour or teacher about their food history. Find out about: their favourite foods as a child; what they associate with different foods, e.g. people, places, times of the year; whether food – or their tastes – have changed since they were young; what they like to eat now; and any other questions you can think of.

Alternatively, imagine that you are a journalist. Decide what interesting questions you would ask a person of your age about the foods they like and why, and whether their favourite foods have always been the same. Record what your own answers would be to these questions.

# Word families

1. Write down all the words you can think of that include the root word *happy*.

   .........................................................................................................................

   .........................................................................................................................

   .........................................................................................................................

2. Write down as many words as you can from the same word class as *happy*. (Clue: is *happy* a noun, verb, adverb or something else?)

   .........................................................................................................................

   .........................................................................................................................

   .........................................................................................................................

3. Write synonyms for the word *happy*.

   .........................................................................................................................

   .........................................................................................................................

   .........................................................................................................................

# The expanding and shrinking sentence!

1. Rewrite each of the sentences below, adding extra detail, for example by using adjectives, adverbs or parenthetical phrases.

   **a** The man walked down the street.

   ...................................................................................................

   ...................................................................................................

   **b** The door opened slowly.

   ...................................................................................................

   ...................................................................................................

   **c** The parrot flew away.

   ...................................................................................................

   ...................................................................................................

2. Rewrite each of the sentences below, to make two or more shorter, clearer sentences.

   **a** The children who were being chased along the beach by their friend ran very fast till they could run no more and then they decided that they would go into the woods so they ran very fast there and then they hid in there and waited until it got dark.

   ...................................................................................................

   ...................................................................................................

   ...................................................................................................

   ...................................................................................................

   **b** Put the butter and sugar into a bowl and stir well until it's fully mixed and really smooth and then add the eggs a bit at a time and beat well until it's really smooth and then stir in the flour until it is all mixed together really well.

   ...................................................................................................

   ...................................................................................................

   ...................................................................................................

   ...................................................................................................

# Effective tweeting

Each of the tweets below indicates a strong opinion about how to eat or exercise. Use what you have learned about topic sentences to respond to each with a single, strong *opposing* point. The first one has been done for you.

a   Shopping in local supermarket today. Astonished to see one man with a trolley full of pizzas.

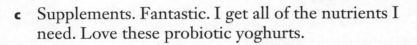

Vegetarian pizzas, which use 50% fat cheese, are an example of popular foods which can be eaten sensibly with care and attention.

b   Never touch breakfast. Worst meal of the day if you want to lose weight.

............................................................................

............................................................................

c   Supplements. Fantastic. I get all of the nutrients I need. Love these probiotic yoghurts.

............................................................................

............................................................................

d   Fast food. Yes, fast way to get out of condition.

............................................................................

............................................................................

e   More sugar in a fizzy drink than in a medium-sized cake. I always drink Zero Sugar.

............................................................................

............................................................................

f   Cinema tonight. Popcorn! What else could it be?

............................................................................

............................................................................

# Spelling bee

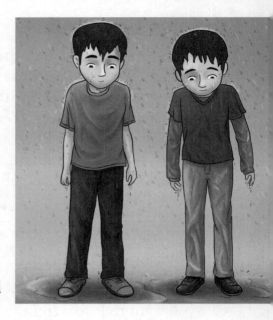

1. Read the sentences below and select the correct spelling for each word with various alternatives.

   **a** On the way home from school, the girls had a big arguement/argumment/argument.

   **b** The experiment basically/basicily/basiccally involves heating the liquid up to see whether it evaporates.

   **c** At the begining/begginning/beginning of the film, the boy runs off into the forest.

   **d** The boys got completely/completly/compleetly drenched in the rain.

   **e** They were very disappointed/dissappointed/disapointed when their football team lost.

   **f** It was the most embarassing/embarrassing/embarrasing day of my entire life!

   **g** The environnment/enviroment/environment is one of the most important topics we study.

   **h** Place the hoops and balls in seperate/separate/separete crates in the gym.

2. Identify five new spellings you need to learn and write down a way of helping you to remember each one, for example, a mnemonic, a picture or a pattern.

   **a** ...........................................................................................................

   ...........................................................................................................

   **b** ...........................................................................................................

   ...........................................................................................................

   **c** ...........................................................................................................

   ...........................................................................................................

   **d** ...........................................................................................................

   ...........................................................................................................

   **e** ...........................................................................................................

   ...........................................................................................................

## Punctuation of sentences

Read the text below.

a Using a pencil, mark the beginning and the end of each sentence.

b In pen, insert capital letters and punctuation to end each sentence.

### Cooking for kids and teens

Cooking for Kids and Teens was started in 2013 by two mums who wanted their kids to learn how to cook and knew they couldn't do it alone it started with two mums and three kids in Laila's kitchen now Cooking for Kids and Teens runs classes across the country click here to find a class near you we want kids and young people to learn how to make simple, wholesome food and understand that FOOD IS FUN our classes for juniors aged 6 to 11 include after school clubs, weekend workshops, preschool 'fun with food' sessions and the very popular day camps for primary kids cooking with new ingredients and flavours will encourage your child to try new foods and expand their diet they will go from cooking simple individual dishes to making a whole meal from scratch we have created special sessions for teens and young adults aged 12 to 16 where they can have fun with friends and learn how to cook well for themselves when they go off to college our classes include guidance on nutrition and hygiene as well as the opportunity to invite friends and family to sample their cooking and admire their skills

## Keeping in touch with friends and family

**1.** Write a short email to a friend to invite him or her to have dinner with your family for a special occasion.

...................................................................................................................

...................................................................................................................

...................................................................................................................

...................................................................................................................

...................................................................................................................

...................................................................................................................

...................................................................................................................

**Remember**

For an informal letter, you need to put your own address, but *not* the address of the person you are writing to. You need to include the date.

**2.** Write a thank you letter to a relative who has given you a very unusual present, which you are not sure you like. Remember your letter should be polite and should show your appreciation.

...................................................................................................................

...................................................................................................................

...................................................................................................................

...................................................................................................................

...................................................................................................................

...................................................................................................................

...................................................................................................................

...................................................................................................................

...................................................................................................................

...................................................................................................................

...................................................................................................................

...................................................................................................................

# Foodies' delight quiz

**1.** Write three synonyms for the word *scared*.

........................................................................................................................................

**2. a** Write a sentence with a co-ordinating conjunction.

........................................................................................................................................

........................................................................................................................................

**b** Write a sentence using a subordinating conjunction.

........................................................................................................................................

........................................................................................................................................

**3.** Expand the following sentence in three different ways:
The mouse ran into a hole.

**a** ...................................................................................

...................................................................................

**b** ...................................................................................

...................................................................................

**c** ...................................................................................

...................................................................................

**4.** State three techniques writers use to keep the reader
interested. For each technique, write an example.

........................................................................................................................................

........................................................................................................................................

........................................................................................................................................

........................................................................................................................................

**5.** How should you start and end:

**a** a personal email or letter to your uncle?

........................................................................................................................................

**b** a formal letter to your local politician?

........................................................................................................................................

## Great writers

William Shakespeare and Charles Dickens are two of literature's greatest writers, but how much do you know about them?

1. Match the statements to the correct author, by drawing lines to link them to the correct picture. There are seven for each one. You may need to do some research.

**William Shakespeare**

Born in Stratford-Upon-Avon in 1564

Born in Portsmouth in 1812

A playwright and poet

Wrote 'Great Expectations'

Had a lifelong fear of being poor

Died in 1616

A novelist

Part-owned The Globe Theatre

Not much is known about his personal life

Died in 1870

Wrote 37 plays

Lived in the Victorian era

Married Anne Hathaway

Many of his novels are about social inequality

**Charles Dickens**

2. How many plays by William Shakespeare and novels by Charles Dickens can you name? Write them below.

<u>Plays by William Shakespeare</u>

<u>Novels by Charles Dickens</u>

......................................................................................        ......................................................................................

......................................................................................        ......................................................................................

......................................................................................        ......................................................................................

......................................................................................        ......................................................................................

......................................................................................        ......................................................................................

......................................................................................        ......................................................................................

......................................................................................        ......................................................................................

# Bias – being assertive

Bias is when a particular subject is preferred over an alternative. It is often used in writing to express a specific point of view and influence the reader to agree.

Being assertive in this context is when you write with a confidence that leads the reader to think what you say is true.

> I can't stand 'Romeo and Juliet'. All that fighting over a pointless argument leaves me with little sympathy for either side. Moreover, the ending must be the most frustrating ever in a play. I really cannot see the appeal of such a grim story.

In the extract above the bias is created by:

- the dismissive tone – 'can't stand' and 'all that fighting'
- the negative assertions – '*pointless* argument'; '*little* sympathy'; '*most frustrating* ever'; '*grim* story'.

1. By changing some key words, the bias can be positive. Rewrite the extract in favour of the play.

   ..............................................................................................................................

   ..............................................................................................................................

   ..............................................................................................................................

   ..............................................................................................................................

2. Here are some assertions that create bias. Place each in the most appropriate box:

   dull and boring     fascinating and complex     rarely encountered worse     a 'must see' event

   completely absorbing     endlessly tiresome     thought-provoking     a magical experience

   completely irrelevant     a new low point     surprisingly engaging     weak and insipid

   | **Positive bias** | **Negative bias** |
   |---|---|
   | | |

13

## Synonyms and antonyms

A word that has a *similar* meaning to another word is called
a synonym.

An antonym is a word that is the *opposite* of another word:

1. Complete the grid below.

| Original word | Synonym | Antonym |
|---|---|---|
| question | query | answer |
| answer | response | |
| strong | | |
| enemy | | |
| begin | | |
| difficult | | |
| angry | | |
| hate | | |
| child | | |
| lose | | |

2. Change the meaning of each sentence by substituting an
   antonym for the underlined word.

   **a**  I would <u>always</u> choose to watch a play by Shakespeare. ..............................................

   **b**  Reading a novel by Charles Dickens is really <u>boring</u>. ..............................................

   **c**  I <u>failed</u> my Shakespeare assignment really <u>badly</u>. ..............................................

   **d**  *Hamlet* remains the <u>least</u> popular Shakespeare play. ..............................................

   **e**  The lead actor was <u>perfect</u> for the role of Hamlet. ..............................................

## Creating a caricature

A caricature is an exaggerated version of a character.

Take Miss Havisham as an example:

- The clocks were stopped at the moment she heard she had been abandoned by her husband-to-be.
- She remains in the same half-dressed state as when she heard the news.
- She has worn the same wedding dress for decades.
- The room she sits in hasn't changed or been cleaned since that day.
- She never leaves her house.
- She hates all men.
- Her skin is as yellow as the once-white dress.

> Miss Havisham

1. List the words you would use to describe Miss Havisham in the box above.

2. Dickens creates memorable characters by exaggerating their appearance and actions.

   Write your own caricature of one of these:

   - a grumpy old lady
   - an angry young man
   - a spoilt child.

   You can use a separate sheet of paper to write down your ideas before beginning your description below.

.............................................................................................................

.............................................................................................................

.............................................................................................................

.............................................................................................................

.............................................................................................................

# Semi-colons

There are three reasons to use a semi-colon:

**A** as a kind of 'super' comma to mark an important break in a sentence

**B** to separate a series of connected issues

**C** to separate two contrasting or balanced clauses.

1. Decide which reason applies in each of these sentences by writing the capital letter in the box.

   **a** Pip is my favourite character in *Great Expectations*; Miss Havisham is the least enjoyable.

   **b** Shakespeare set these plays in Italy: *Romeo and Juliet*, which is a tragedy; *The Two Gentlemen of Verona*, a comedy; *Much Ado About Nothing*, a comedy; and *The Tempest*, which is also classed as a comedy but is sometimes referred to as a romance.

   **c** I was told by a friend I wouldn't like *Hamlet*; I won't listen to him again!

   **d** These are my favourite quotations from Shakespeare's work: 'To be or not to be' from *Hamlet*; 'All the world's a stage and all the men and women merely players' from *As You Like It*; 'Now is the winter of our discontent' from *Richard III*; and 'What's in a name? That which we call a rose by any other name would smell as sweet' from *Romeo and Juliet*.

2. Now it is your turn to write three sentences, each showing a different use of semi-colons.

   Sentence 1: ................................................................................

   ................................................................................

   ................................................................................

   Sentence 2: ................................................................................

   ................................................................................

   ................................................................................

   Sentence 3: ................................................................................

   ................................................................................

   ................................................................................

# Creating atmosphere in your writing

Read this short extract from another novel by
Charles Dickens.

> Fog everywhere. Fog up the river, where it flows among green
> aits and meadows; fog down the river, where it rolls defiled
> among the tiers of shipping and the waterside pollutions of
> a great (and dirty) city. Fog on the Essex marshes, fog on the
> Kentish heights (...) Fog in the eyes and throats of ancient
> Greenwich pensioners, wheezing by the firesides of their wards;
> fog in the stem and bowl of the afternoon pipe of the wrathful
> skipper, down in his close cabin; fog cruelly pinching the toes
> and fingers of his shivering little 'prentice boy on deck. Chance
> people on the bridges peeping over the parapets into a nether sky
> of fog, with fog all round them, as if they were up in a balloon
> and hanging in the misty clouds.
>
> From *Bleak House* by Charles Dickens

It is not necessary to understand every reference in the extract
to work out the atmosphere Dickens has created.

**1.** How many times is the word *fog* used in the extract?

.........................................................................................................................................

**2.** Think of how fog seems to drift into every place possible.
List three people and three locations the fog encounters.

.........................................................................................................................................

.........................................................................................................................................

**3.** Choose one of the following kinds of day:
- rainy
- snowy
- windy
- sunny

Write the first three sentences of a description of your chosen
kind of day, concentrating on creating a suitable atmosphere.

.........................................................................................................................................

.........................................................................................................................................

.........................................................................................................................................

.........................................................................................................................................

## Writing a playscript – adapting a story

Playscripts are set out differently to works of prose:

- Each character speaks in turn in a dialogue.
- There is no narrative description.
- There is no need to use speech marks.
- Stage directions guide the actors' performance.

Adapt the extract below into a playscript. Pip is standing before Miss Haversham in her living room. The opening two lines have been completed for you.

"Who is it?" said the lady at the table.

"Pip, ma'am."

"Pip?"

"Mr. Pumblechook's boy, ma'am. Come – to play."

"Come nearer; let me look at you. Come close."

It was when I stood before her, avoiding her eyes, that I took note of the surrounding objects in detail, and saw that her watch had stopped at twenty minutes to nine, and that a clock in the room had stopped at twenty minutes to nine.

"Look at me," said Miss Havisham. "You are not afraid of a woman who has never seen the sun since you were born?"

I regret to state that I was not afraid of telling the enormous lie comprehended in the answer "No."

"Do you know what I touch here?" she said, laying her hands, one upon the other, on her left side.

"Yes, ma'am." (It made me think of the young man.)

"What do I touch?"

"Your heart."

"Broken!"

From *Great Expectations* by Charles Dickens

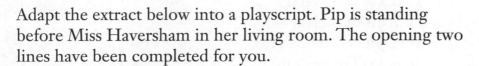

Miss Havisham: (*sitting at the table*) Who is it?

Pip: (*standing nervously*) Pip, ma'am.

....................................................................................................................

....................................................................................................................

....................................................................................................................

....................................................................................................................

....................................................................................................................

....................................................................................................................

## Amazing arts quiz

**1.** 'Born in 1564, died in 1616 and the writer of 37 plays'
Who is this describing?

..................................................................................................

**2.** 'Never before have I read such an amazing novel. It will
keep you entertained for hours.'
Why is this writing biased?

..................................................................................................

..................................................................................................

**3.** What is the main difference between a synonym and
an antonym?

..................................................................................................

..................................................................................................

**4.** Why is Miss Havisham a caricature?

..................................................................................................

**5.** When might you use a semi-colon?

..................................................................................................

..................................................................................................

**6.** What technique does Dickens use to create the
atmosphere in the following extract?

> Fog creeping into the cabooses of collier-brigs; fog lying out
> on the yards and hovering in the rigging of great ships; fog
> drooping on the gunwales of barges and small boats.
> From *Bleak House* by Charles Dickens

..................................................................................................

..................................................................................................

**7.** Which four verbs help to create the atmosphere in the
above extract from *Bleak House*?

..................................................................................................

**8.** What are four key features of a playscript?

..................................................................................................

..................................................................................................

# 3 Terrific technology

## Technology for us all

Technology has advanced rapidly over the last half century.

The humble household electric vacuum cleaner is credited as one of the great inventions of the 20th century, but did you know that the idea of using a vacuum goes back to the mid-1600s? Of course, the modern contemporary machine is a world away from its distant cousin. You can now buy a robot vacuum cleaner that works independently and uses sensors to avoid crashing into the furniture. It must work, as thousands have been sold since it went into production in 2002. If you look online, there are all kinds of vacuum cleaners for different flooring, depending on whether you have pets or not and how big your house is.

Choose any piece of technology you have at home.

1. In less than 100 words, describe your chosen piece of technology, explaining its purpose and functions.

   .....................................................................................................................
   .....................................................................................................................
   .....................................................................................................................
   .....................................................................................................................
   .....................................................................................................................

2. Research how your piece of technology has changed in the last few decades. Write five main differences as bullet points.

   - .................................................................................................................
   - .................................................................................................................
   - .................................................................................................................
   - .................................................................................................................
   - .................................................................................................................

3. Are the above changes all advantages?

   .....................................................................................................................
   .....................................................................................................................
   .....................................................................................................................

# Regular and irregular verbs

Regular verbs are those that follow conventional rules when conjugated (e.g. changed to another tense). Irregular verbs break the rules.

| Present tense | Past tense | Future tense | Regular/ Irregular |
|---|---|---|---|
| open | opened | will open | regular |
| understand | **understood** | will understand | irregular |

Complete the table below.

| Present tense | Past tense | Future tense | Regular/Irregular |
|---|---|---|---|
| take | took | will take | irregular |
| swarm | | | regular |
| copy | copied | | |
| | | will drink | |
| | wrote | | |
| bring | | | |
| teach | | | |
| study | | | |
| stare | | | |
| complete | | | |
| | broke | | |

# Questions and answers

There are lots of different kinds of questions:

**Open questions** – *How are you?*

**Closed questions** – *How old are you?*

**Leading questions** – *Why is that TV show so bad?*

**Rhetorical questions** – *You don't want that, do you?*

There are also different kinds of answers. Here are six.

| | |
|---|---|
| Partial answer | Direct response |
| No response | Misdirection |
| Avoidance | A lie |

1.  Several people were asked the question: Would you trust a robot in your home? Here are the responses. Decide what kind they are. The first one is done for you.

    a   No, I wouldn't!                                    Direct response

    b   The homeowner stated, "I don't have a home." ....................................................

    c   Er, could you repeat the question? ....................................................

    d   I refuse to answer that question. ....................................................

    e   Don't you think they're really ugly? ....................................................

    f   Maybe, it depends. ....................................................

    g   I think robots are so expensive. ....................................................

2.  In most stories, robots are programmed to tell the truth because it is more logical to do so. If this is true, which of the six kinds of responses above is a robot capable of giving? ....................................................

3.  Identify the following types of question.

    a   Can you repair that robot? ....................................................

    b   Isn't it wonderful that we have a robot to clean the kitchen? ....................................................

    c   If you didn't have a robot, you wouldn't have so much free time, would you? ....................................................

    d   What would happen if robots became more intelligent than people? ....................................................

# Using subject-specific words

Always try to use technical vocabulary linked to the subject you are writing about in order to:

- show your specific knowledge of the subject
- inform and instruct the reader
- be accurate.

Read this extract:

> Roboticists within the robotics field of science have disagreed over the moral question of artificial intelligence for decades. Some have argued that the neural pathways in the positronic brain make robots much more dependable because they aren't capable of lying. Others have countered that, by using 264-bit binary code programming, the neurons in the artificial neural network can be taught to make the robot autonomous.

**1.** There are ten subject-specific technical terms in the passage. Can you find them?

.................................................... ....................................................

.................................................... ....................................................

.................................................... ....................................................

.................................................... ....................................................

.................................................... ....................................................

**2.** Which technical term appears twice?

....................................................................................................................

**3.** Why do you think it appears twice?

....................................................................................................................

....................................................................................................................

**4.** Now it is your turn to create a technical vocabulary. Choose an area of science or technology you know, such as physics, chemistry, biology, computing.

Write at least ten technical terms. If you can find twenty, you're an expert!

....................................................

....................................................

....................................................

....................................................

....................................................

# Fitting sentences to purpose

You can control pace, tone, atmosphere and how much you want the reader to know through your sentence construction.

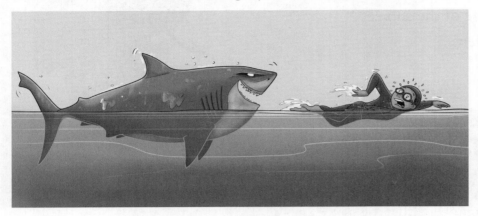

1. Read the text below and write a sentence better suited to that purpose.

   Excuse me, please, but I am in need of assistance. I appear to be in danger of being eaten by this very large shark swimming at a fast pace towards my current position. I believe scientists call it 'Carcharodon Carcharias' but you would know it as a 'Great White'. I can tell this by the size of its mouth and the number of teeth closing in on me.

2. Aanjay is trying to write a scientific report on an incident in a laboratory but it needs a lot more information.

   Help him by adding more information to each box.

   It was yesterday.

   I was doing an experiment.

   It went wrong.

   I'm okay but the lab isn't.

# Words with similar meanings

Each word in the English language has its own individual definition but often there are words with a similar meaning that can be grouped together. These are called synonyms.

Take the word *aeroplane* as an example:

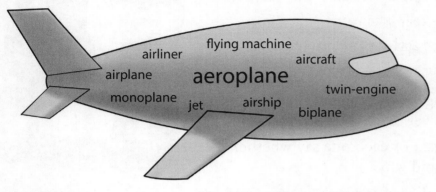

**1.** Add at least five synonyms to each box, but aim for ten each.

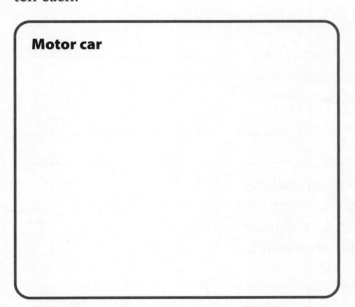

**Motor car**

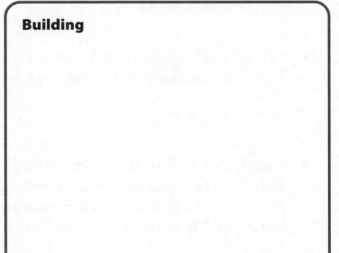

**Building**

**2.** Underline the words which do not belong in this group.

| star | galaxy | Milky Way | orbit | moon | submarine | sun |
| --- | --- | --- | --- | --- | --- | --- |

weather      asteroids      atmosphere      aeroplane      comet      meteor

cosmic      constellation      horoscope      ocean

The group theme is ............................................................................. .

## Writing the opening of a speech

This is an effective opening from a speech made by a salesman selling robots:

> "How many times have you wished for a magic wand to do all your jobs around the house? Why is it you have to look after your baby sister at exactly the time your friends call? Who hasn't wished they had more 'me' time? If these scenarios apply to you then I have the perfect solution. Meet Robot 101 – your new best friend."

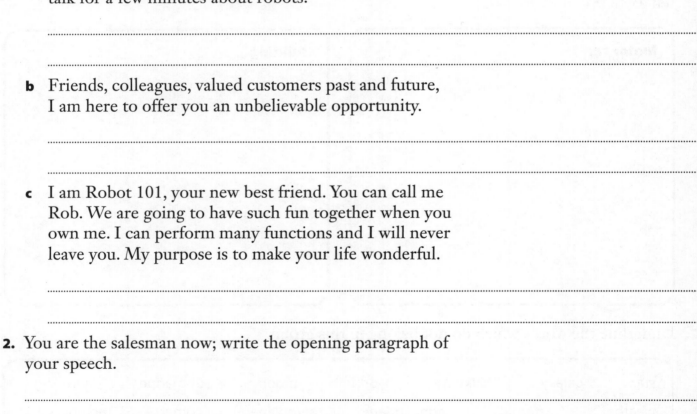

It begins by asking questions to engage the audience before introducing the product as the answer to all your problems.

1. Here are some more beginnings. For each one say whether you think it is effective or not, and why.

   **a** I haven't really prepared anything but I suppose I could talk for a few minutes about robots.

   ........................................................................................

   ........................................................................................

   **b** Friends, colleagues, valued customers past and future, I am here to offer you an unbelievable opportunity.

   ........................................................................................

   ........................................................................................

   **c** I am Robot 101, your new best friend. You can call me Rob. We are going to have such fun together when you own me. I can perform many functions and I will never leave you. My purpose is to make your life wonderful.

   ........................................................................................

   ........................................................................................

2. You are the salesman now; write the opening paragraph of your speech.

   ........................................................................................

   ........................................................................................

   ........................................................................................

   ........................................................................................

   ........................................................................................

# Terrific technology quiz

1.  Why would you ever want to own a robot?

    What kind of question is this? Does it need an answer?

    ..................................................................................................................................

2.  What is the difference between a regular and an irregular verb?

    ..................................................................................................................................

    ..................................................................................................................................

3.  Do you agree that GM crops are dangerous? Answer this question using:

    **a** a direct response: ...................................................................................

    **b** a misdirection: ........................................................................................

4.  Add three more examples to expand this grouping of subject-specific terms related to growing crops: *tillage; crop rotation; planting; ploughing; irrigating; fertilising.*

    ..................................................................................................................................

5.  Which sentence is more suitable for its purpose? Why?

    **a** It may be a good time to tell everyone that I have made a rather large mistake when mixing the chemicals for my experiment and it seems there has been a somewhat violent reaction which could cause a major incident that threatens both us and the laboratory.

    **b** Run, the lab's going to explode!

    ..................................................................................................................................

6.  Connect these synonyms to make matching pairs.

    robot            satellite

    moon             missile

    planet           meteor

    falling star     world

    rocket           android

7.  Why is this effective as an opening to a speech?

    "Isn't it remarkable that we still don't know enough about GM crops? With all this scientific knowledge, we are still no nearer to knowing if they will cause long-term harm. Doesn't this make you feel somewhat uneasy? I know I feel that way."

    ..................................................................................................................................

    ..................................................................................................................................

## Debating

Here's your chance to have another go at debating. You'll need at least one other person to prepare a speech opposing what you say.

You can choose your own motion, but here are some ideas to help you.

- Homework is of no use to anybody.
- The law should be reformed to allow people to drive at 12 years old.
- There are too many rules and regulations in our country.

Now prepare some brief notes to remind you what you will say. Think of at least three arguments and work out how you would explain each one.

**Argument 1** ...........................................................

.................................................................................

.................................................................................

**Explanation** ...........................................................

.................................................................................

.................................................................................

**Argument 2** ...........................................................

.................................................................................

.................................................................................

**Explanation** ...........................................................

.................................................................................

.................................................................................

**Argument 3** ...........................................................

.................................................................................

.................................................................................

**Explanation** ...........................................................

.................................................................................

.................................................................................

**Argument 4** ...........................................................

.................................................................................

.................................................................................

**Explanation** ...........................................................

.................................................................................

.................................................................................

How I will end my speech: ....................................................................

...........................................................................................................

...........................................................................................................

# Writing a letter

Mary Kingsley was a remarkable woman. She died over a hundred years ago, but if she were alive today she would be greatly admired.

Here is another very brief extract from Mary's journal.

It was a wonderfully lovely quiet night with no light save that from the stars. (...) I paddled leisurely across the lake to the shore on the right, and seeing crawling on the ground some large glow-worms, drove the canoe on to the bank among some hippo grass, and got out to get them. (...) I felt the earth quiver under my feet, and heard a soft big soughing sound, and looking round saw I had dropped in on a hippo banquet. I made out five of the immense brutes round me, so I softly returned to the canoe and shoved off (...)

Imagine Mary Kingsley is still alive. Write her a letter inviting her to come to talk to the students in your school. You should aim to write three paragraphs. State your reason for writing, why you think the students would enjoy hearing her speak and giving a brief plan for her visit.

Dear Mary Kingsley,

...................................................................................................................................

...................................................................................................................................

...................................................................................................................................

...................................................................................................................................

...................................................................................................................................

...................................................................................................................................

...................................................................................................................................

...................................................................................................................................

...................................................................................................................................

...................................................................................................................................

...................................................................................................................................

Yours sincerely,

## Know which tense to use

**1.** Using the simple present tense, continue this advice from a teacher.

"Claudia, I try my best to teach you English, but every day you come into the classroom and just don't concentrate. When I ask you to get your book out, you ........................................................................................

................................................................................................................................

................................................................................................................................

..........................................................................................................."

**2.** Now use the simple past as if you were observing the lesson.

Claudia listened quietly to her teacher and then nodded her head and smiled a little smile. ........................................................................................

................................................................................................................................

................................................................................................................................

.............................................................................................................................. .

**3.** Pretend you are Claudia and you have just got home from school. Finish this entry in your diary, using the present continuous tense.

I am sitting by my window, drinking a glass of lovely pineapple juice. The birds in the garden are singing sweetly ................................................

................................................................................................................................

................................................................................................................................

.............................................................................................................................. .

**4.** Now pretend to be Claudia's parent telling the teacher the following day how Claudia had explained her lack of attention in the lesson. Use the past continuous tense.

"Claudia told us last night that she was struggling to focus because ............

................................................................................................................................

................................................................................................................................

.........................................................................................................." .

# Reading about settings

Read these tips for visitors to the Arctic and answer the questions.

Don't get me wrong, because the tundra is not the most dangerous holiday destination, but there are three things you should look out for. The first is a whiteout. You can be walking down the street when out of nowhere a snowstorm envelopes you. Everything turns white and you can only see a few centimetres in front of you. You are instantly disoriented and the temperature plummets to -50 degrees Celsius. And that's only in town. Another problem is the polar bear. No, he is not friendly at all, and attacks by polar bears are usually fatal – for humans. People who live near the bears usually go about in groups and always, repeat always, carry rifles. Good luck! Finally, if you want a comfortable night's rest, beware of mosquitoes and black flies. If you go where the mosquitoes hang out, you need long-sleeved shirts and tough trousers, and you should make sure you have a good-quality insect repellent. Otherwise, welcome to the tundra!

**1.** List three things people should be careful of when they go to the tundra.

.................................................................................................................................

**2.** What do you think a whiteout is?

.................................................................................................................................

**3.** Which word indicates that it suddenly gets very cold? Check the spelling.

.................................................................................................................................

**4.** Which word indicates that you have no idea where you are? Check the spelling.

.................................................................................................................................

**5.** Why does the speaker say "good-quality" when he describes insect repellent?

.................................................................................................................................

**6.** Why might you be convinced that polar bears are seriously dangerous?

.................................................................................................................................

**7.** Why or why not would you enjoy visiting the tundra?

.................................................................................................................................

.................................................................................................................................

## Using conditional sentences

Here are some ideas for you to think about.

- If animals could speak ................................................................................................................
- If dinosaurs ruled the world ......................................................................................................
- If children were in charge of everything ..............................................................................
- If I can ................................................................................................................, you can.
- If it doesn't stop raining ...........................................................................................................

Write your ideas below.

### If only...

- If only I were two metres tall ..................................................................................................

.............................................................................................................................................

- If only you were a millionaire ..................................................................................................

.............................................................................................................................................

- If only we had not got locked in at school ..........................................................................

.............................................................................................................................................

- ................................................................................ there'd be enough food

for everyone in the world and no more starvation.

- ................................................................................ there'd be no more war.

### What if...

- What if we all decided to turn up to school ten minutes late?

.............................................................................................................................................

- What if I had been more helpful when my aunt was so busy?

.............................................................................................................................................

Now practise making your own sentences using *if*.

.............................................................................................................................................

.............................................................................................................................................

.............................................................................................................................................

# Image explorer

```
                    ┌──────────────────┐
                    │  Image explorer  │
                    └──────────────────┘
```

Simile – *like a silver dart*

Metaphor – *the trees were a smudge on the sand*

Personification – *night wears a black cloak and hides behind buildings*

What images can you use to make these ideas stand out more clearly? Try to use a simile, a metaphor and personification for each scene.

The sounds in a busy market ..................................................................................

...........................................................................................................................

...........................................................................................................................

A fast-growing creeper in the jungle ......................................................................

...........................................................................................................................

...........................................................................................................................

Picking up something unpleasant by mistake .........................................................

...........................................................................................................................

...........................................................................................................................

The Arctic Circle .................................................................................................

...........................................................................................................................

...........................................................................................................................

Someone's room after a burglar has broken in ......................................................

...........................................................................................................................

...........................................................................................................................

A scene of your own connected with nature ...........................................................

...........................................................................................................................

...........................................................................................................................

## Writing a summary

"Mum, there was this man told us all about kangaroos and their babies –
Joeys they're called. I didn't know you could eat kangaroos – I think it's cruel,
but the man says there's very little fat. Mind you, there are 34 million of them
in Australia – that's where they live. Joeys live in a pouch on their mum's
front. Did you know they can leap along at 20 to 25 kilometres per hour? He
said they are shy animals and they are nocturnal and come out at night. They
come from a family that means big foot. I suppose that's why they can leap
along so fast. And they can swim!"

The student did well to remember all this information, but
there's no order to it. Can you get 11 facts into some sort of
order to write a clear summary?

There are 108 words. Aim to write 60– 65 words for your
summary.

**Notes**

Fact 1: ......................................................................................................

Fact 2: ......................................................................................................

Fact 3: ......................................................................................................

Fact 4: ......................................................................................................

Fact 5: ......................................................................................................

Fact 6: ......................................................................................................

Fact 7: ......................................................................................................

Fact 8: ......................................................................................................

Fact 9: ......................................................................................................

Fact 10: ....................................................................................................

Fact 11: ....................................................................................................

My summary: ............................................................................................

...................................................................................................................

...................................................................................................................

...................................................................................................................

Word count: .............................................................................................

## Unnatural nature quiz

1. What are two good topics for a debate?

   **a** ..............................................................................................................................

   **b** ..............................................................................................................................

2. What tense is the following sentence using?

   I am sitting here watching the elephants soaking themselves with water.

   **a** Past continuous               **c** Simple present

   **b** Present continuous         **d** Simple past

3. Write a sentence about dolphins using the past continuous tense.

   ..................................................................................................................................

4. In 30 seconds, write down 10 words associated with cold.

   **a** .......................................................     **f** .......................................................

   **b** .......................................................     **g** .......................................................

   **c** .......................................................     **h** .......................................................

   **d** .......................................................     **i** .......................................................

   **e** .......................................................     **j** .......................................................

5. What two words in this list mean roughly the same thing: *hollow, oval-shaped, crescent, elliptical, circular*? Underline them.

6. Which of these *if* sentences is definite, which is likely and which is improbable? Write 'D', 'L' or 'I' next to each.

   **a** If we get too close to that whale, it will scare us. ..........................

   **b** If that whale splashes us, we will get wet. ..........................

   **c** If I'd known we were going to see a whale, I'd have died. ..................

7. Put these in order of which you think best personifies the sea.

   **a** A monster            **c** An angel

   **b** An angry soldier     **d** An old man

8. List three things you must *not* do when writing a summary.

   ..................................................................................................................................

   ..................................................................................................................................

## Market research

If you were to write your own magazine, you would need to do some research and planning.

Like any writer, you need to make your product appealing to your target audience.

### Research

1. Study two magazines aimed at a teenage audience. Fill out this table based on your findings by ticking which features are in each magazine.

| | Features found in first magazine | Features found in second magazine |
|---|---|---|
| Engaging front cover | | |
| Bold, easy-to-spot title | | |
| Index of features | | |
| Mixture of fonts | | |
| Colour images | | |
| Editorials | | |
| Reviews | | |
| Reports | | |
| Interviews | | |
| Human interest articles | | |
| Topical articles | | |
| Advertisements | | |
| Letters page | | |
| Games page | | |
| Horoscopes | | |

### Planning

2. Based on your research, make a list of the contents you think should be included in your school sports and hobbies magazine.

.................................................................................................................

.................................................................................................................

.................................................................................................................

# Some facts about kayaks

Articles in magazines often introduce unusual topics and offer a mixture of facts and opinions. Sometimes the opinions are presented as facts to persuade the reader. Such articles aim to be informative and inspiring.

Here is an extract from an article about the benefits of trying new outdoor sports.

To those who are ignorant of the finer details, all kayaks may seem to be the same. In fact, there are different types of kayak, designed for various water conditions and the level of expertise of the individual kayaker. Sit-on-top kayaks remain the most popular for beginners and are intended for use on flat stretches of water, whilst more experienced kayakers prefer the cockpit kind in which the legs are covered by a watertight canopy.

Indeed, kayaks have come a long way from their original use as vessels for hunting and travelling, as used by the Inuit tribes of the ancient Arctic region some four millennia ago. Now they are used as vessels for sport in all kinds of water. Sea kayaks, white water kayaks and river kayaks are just three variations on the theme. Whatever you decide, kayaking is an exhilarating and rewarding experience.

**1.** Identify an opinion in the first paragraph that is presented as a fact.

.......................................................................................................................

**2.** Find three facts in the first paragraph.

.......................................................................................................................

.......................................................................................................................

.......................................................................................................................

**3.** In your opinion, how relevant and useful is the information in the second  paragraph? Give reasons for your answer.

.......................................................................................................................

.......................................................................................................................

.......................................................................................................................

**4.** What impact might the last sentence have on the reader?

.......................................................................................................................

.......................................................................................................................

## Using the prefix *in-*

The prefix *in-* usually changes the meaning of a word to its opposite meaning. For example:

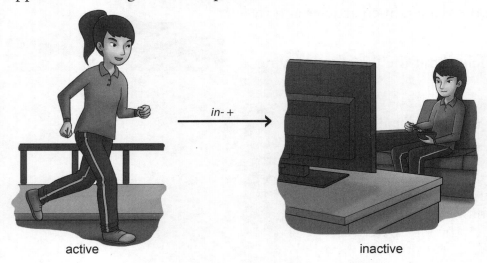

active                                                          inactive

Look at the following words and read sentences 1–6 below.
Then choose the best word to fill in each of the gaps.

- inactivity
- inconsiderate
- indecision
- independent

- insecure
- insincere
- insufficient

1. The team lost because of too much

   .................................................................................................................................

2. A round-the-world yachtsman needs to be

   .................................................................................................................................

3. .................................................... is a state of doing nothing, which
   leads to a lack of fitness.

4. No one believed the tennis star as he was being

   .................................................................................................................................

5. The defence conceded five goals because it was

   .................................................................................................................................

6. The club could not pay the players' wages because there

   were .................................................... funds.

# Using vocabulary for effect

The effect a writer wants to create is linked to the point of view being expressed. This is the perspective and will differ depending on the bias of the writer.

Read these two perspectives on the same subject.

---

**A** I find stamp collecting to be a most intriguing and rewarding hobby. Each stamp has its own unique and captivating history that is both informative and entertaining in equal measures. In addition, I have met many fellow philatelists who themselves are fascinating characters with countless appealing tales to tell.

---

**B** Never in all my days have I come across a more pointless, boring and mind-numbing hobby than collecting stamps. Paying huge amounts of hard-earned money for tatty pieces of second-hand paper seems to me an exercise in futility. It is a hobby for anti-social and uninteresting people. Who in their right mind wants to learn about stamps anyway?

---

**1.** Create your own positive and negative word clouds by choosing words and phrases from the extracts.

| **Positive** | **Negative** |
|---|---|
|  |  |

**2.** Choose a sport or hobby that you either strongly like or strongly dislike. Write a descriptive paragraph from your biased perspective.

......................................................................................................................................

......................................................................................................................................

......................................................................................................................................

......................................................................................................................................

......................................................................................................................................

## Using punctuation accurately

### Colons

Colons are used to introduce an example or explanation within a sentence. They are also used to introduce a list.

1. Desiree is having problems with her use of colons. Can you help her by adding the correct punctuation below?

   a Ever since I was a child I have listened to all kinds of music slow fast modern and old-style.

   b It would be wonderful if I could meet my favourite rock star I would be overawed.

   c To start a band you need guitars keyboards drums and a singer.

   d I love the sound of a steel guitar it is so relaxing.

   e I've played live concerts in all the world's major cities London Cairo New York Mumbai Moscow.

### Brackets and dashes

Brackets (parentheses) and dashes can be used to add extra information to sentences and – in addition – dashes can create a change of emphasis.

2. Copy these sentences but add brackets or dashes where appropriate.

   a Beyoncé was born in Houston Texas but has moved to Los Angeles California having once lived in New York.

   ............................................................................................................

   ............................................................................................................

   b She is a now a solo artist having made her name in the group Destiny's Child and has sold over 75 million records worldwide.

   ............................................................................................................

   ............................................................................................................

   c Beyoncé a leading figure in the music industry has won many music awards.

   ............................................................................................................

   ............................................................................................................

# When to write informally

Magazines are a mixture of formal and informal written pieces.

**1.** Match the type of writing to the purpose and decide whether it is formal, informal or both.

| Feature | Purpose | Formal or informal? |
| --- | --- | --- |
| Editorial | Offers opinion on topic | Formal |
| Index of features | | |
| Review | | |
| Letters page | | |
| Advertisements | | |
| Reports | | |
| Interviews | | |
| Articles | | |

The letters page may be more informal in both style and appearance. Here is an example:

Dear Sel, I'm having real trouble convincing my dad that he should let me try trial biking. I've seen it on TV and it looks so cool. I don't care about falling off but me dad says it's a fool's sport and there's no way he wants me to end up in hospital. What can I do? All me mates are doin' it and I'm sitting at home writing letters. Please, please help me!!!

**2.** What features of the writing tell you this is an informal piece?

...........................................................................................................................

...........................................................................................................................

**3.** Write a reply in a similar informal style.

...........................................................................................................................

...........................................................................................................................

...........................................................................................................................

...........................................................................................................................

## Writing a review

This extract is from a formal review with a clear perspective.

> When it first appeared, the Xbox One was to many a huge disappointment. Overpriced and underpowered, it was no match for the rival PS4. Where Sony had delivered, Microsoft had failed. For all its hype and range of advanced features, the Xbox could not compete at the most basic level against the PS4 – as a games console it came second every time.
>
> Now let us move forward in time to the present. What a transformation has occurred! No longer the poor little sibling, the Xbox has found its feet and become the alpha male the company promised it would be. More powerful, less expensive and, with a quality controller, the vision has come to fruition.

1. According to the review, what were the original problems with the Xbox One?

   ................................................................................................................................

2. How did it compare with the PS4 as a games console?

   ................................................................................................................................

3. Why is it now a better games console?

   ................................................................................................................................

4. What is the perspective (angle) that the writer uses?

   ................................................................................................................................

5. Now it is your turn to write a review. You can choose from a film, book, TV show, computer game or console, or any subject connected to hobbies.

   My review of ................................................................................................................

   ................................................................................................................................

   ................................................................................................................................

   ................................................................................................................................

   ................................................................................................................................

   ................................................................................................................................

   ................................................................................................................................

# Fabulous hobbies quiz

**1.** Which of these features in a magazine should be written in a more formal writing style and which in an informal style? Place either an 'F' or an 'I' alongside each feature.

Editorials ..........          Interviews ..........          Advertisements ..........

Reviews ..........          Human interest articles ..........          Letters page ..........

Reports ..........          Topical articles ..........          Games page ..........

**2.** Underline the statement that is an opinion stated as a fact.

**a** Kayaking is a really exciting sport to participate in.

**b** Different kinds of kayaks are used for different water conditions.

**c** Most kayakers are people who want to push themselves to the limits of their abilities.

**d** I think kayaking is great fun and a good way to spend the weekend.

**3.** What do you think the following idiom means?

It was a game of two halves.

........................................................................................................................................................

**4.** Underline the six words that create a positive perspective in the following sentences.

Walking delights me. I love to spend the day freely wandering the magnificent hills near my home. I am blessed to have such a marvellous resource so close by.

**5.** Add the correct punctuation to the sentence below.

These four clubs were founding members of the Premier League Liverpool, Manchester United Arsenal and Chelsea.

**6.** Which of these features is not typical of a review? Underline your answer.

**a** A clear perspective or angle          **d** A judgement

**b** A question and answer section          **e** Quotations

**c** Formal writing

**7.** Give two reasons why you would use a dash in a sentence.

........................................................................................................................................................

........................................................................................................................................................

# 6 Alarming journeys

## Discussing journeys

Find two or three people to share a discussion. Choose one of the three journeys below and discuss how you think the journey might be difficult or scary.

Before you start your discussion, you might wish to make brief notes of your ideas to share.

A climb you might go on

......................................................................................................

......................................................................................................

A journey involving water

......................................................................................................

......................................................................................................

A journey to a new city or town

......................................................................................................

......................................................................................................

......................................................................................................

Be prepared to give a summary of your discussion to the class.

# Unpacking words

Some words are like parcels: they have different layers of meaning to be unpacked.

When you hear a word, it makes you think of other things. When you are writing, this helps you to choose the word you want. When you are reading, it prompts your imagination.

For example, think about noises. To start you off, here's a very simple sentence:

The creature made a noise.

1. Read the following sentences, which use more powerful words than *noise*. Write single words or short phrases to describe what you imagine when you read them.

   **a** The creature growled. ......................................................................

   **b** It groaned. ......................................................................

   **c** There was a buzzing. ......................................................................

   **d** It whimpered. ......................................................................

   **e** At night I heard howling in the wood. ......................................................................

   **f** For an answer he just grunted. ......................................................................

   **g** Year 8, what is this cacophony? ......................................................................

   **h** Stop grumbling! ......................................................................

   **i** A twittering came from the box. ......................................................................

   **j** Cackling, she turned slowly. ......................................................................

2. Write a sentence or two to describe the sounds of a large, violent and angry animal that has just become aware of your presence.

......................................................................

......................................................................

......................................................................

......................................................................

......................................................................

......................................................................

## A prepositional verse

Sometimes you can put several prepositional phrases together, a bit like joining pieces of string – although this can get rather clumsy.

1.  Here's a verse made almost entirely out of prepositional phrases. Choose an appropriate preposition to go at the beginning of each line. All the prepositions could be different.

> I met a creature
>
> .............................. the top step
>
> .............................. the staircase
>
> .............................. the carpet
>
> .............................. six creepy-crawly legs
>
> .............................. five centimetres long
>
> I took it
>
> .............................. its hiding place
>
> .............................. my shaking hand
>
> .............................. greatest peril
>
> .............................. my fragile sanity
>
> I couldn't bear to kill it so it went
>
> .............................. a pretty little box
>
> .............................. the windowsill
>
> .............................. the floral curtains
>
> .............................. some later time
>
> My annoying little sister happened to find the box and, being inquisitive, had to discover what was in it.
>
> Ha! Ha! Very ha, ha!

2.  Try writing your own verse using a string of prepositional phrases.

.............................................................................................................

.............................................................................................................

.............................................................................................................

.............................................................................................................

.............................................................................................................

## Making a big splash!

What is the difference between an object hitting the water and making the droplets fly everywhere and a ripe peach dropped onto a concrete path?

Answer: one goes 'splash!' and the other goes 'splat!'

Think about the sound *spla*. Why does one word end in *–sh* and the other in *–t*? They're both examples of onomatopoeia – they sound like what is happening.

1. Here's another example for you to work out.

   Say *push* and *pull* several times slowly. Act the movements out by swaying your body in time to the two words. What happens in your mouth when you say these words? How are they different?

   ...................................................................................................................................................

   ...................................................................................................................................................

2. This is part of a poem about the sounds made by instruments in a jazz band.

   Underline the words that you think are examples of onomatopoeia and discuss why you have chosen them.

   **Jazz Fantasia**

   Drum on your drums, batter on your banjoes,
   sob on the long cool winding saxophones.

   Go to it, O jazzmen.

   Sling your knuckles on the bottoms of the happy
   tin pans, let your trombones ooze, and go husha-
   husha-hush with the slippery sand-paper.

   From 'Jazz Fantasia' by Carl Sandburg

## Crossword puzzle

There are 14 words in this crossword puzzle that come from the poem 'In the wake of the Fram'. The first clue has been done for you.

We recommend that you read the poem once, and quickly, and then try see how many clues you can answer without looking at the poem a second time.

Across

1. The path taken by the boat, contrasted to a mountain (6,5)

2. Onomatopoeic word used to describe the rain (8)

3. A piece of broken ice, with a sharp edge (5)

4. Describes how the crew felt while the boat was in a slew (8)

5. Emotion shown by the crew on arriving at their destination (7)

6. Verb to describe that the Captain feels momentarily falters (7)

Down

1. Another word used for the boat (4)

2. Conveys the nervous anticipation of the crew (8).

3. Another word used for the boat (3)

4. Term used to describe pleasant weather (9)

5. Adjective used for the exhilarated crew as they recall the original voyage (5)

6. Small white crystals on the boat (5)

7. Verb used to describe the noise made by the boat (4)

8. Time in months that the crew were in difficult waters (5)

How many answers did you get?

Now go ahead and look at the poem and complete the crossword.

## Creative writing

Some students have to take dangerous journeys to school. Imagine that you lived in a village that was cut off and that you and your friends have to cross a perilous bridge to get to school. Write about your first experience of doing this. How did you feel as you began the crossing, what happened and how did you feel when you got to the other side?

# Responding to a poem

Read the following poem, where the poet journeys back to the local market she visited as a child and reflects on how much it has changed. Answer the questions that follow.

**Hungry Ghost**

Today I went shopping with my father
after many years. I was back
in time to when I'd follow Grandfather
to the market, smelling the spicy scents,
drinking the sights and mingling with the shouts.
Neither buyer nor seller, I would float
like a restless spirit hungry for life.

The market is bigger. I have grown too.
There are more goods as distances have shrunk.
The prices are higher. I understand
about money and, alas, its bondage
of buyers and sellers. Almost I wish
I was again that hungry ghost, watchful
and floating through the world's noisy bazaar.

'Hungry Ghost' by Debjani Chatterjee

**Remember**

A metaphor is used to represent someone or something as something else.

1. How does the poet describe the atmosphere at the market in the first verse? Use examples to support your answer.

   .................................................................................................................

   .................................................................................................................

2. The last line of the poem refers to the 'world's noisy bazaar'. What might this metaphor mean?

   .................................................................................................................

   .................................................................................................................

3. What is the poet's wish at the end of the poem?

   .................................................................................................................

   .................................................................................................................

# Alarming journeys quiz

**1.** Look at the words below. What do they mean and how are they different? Fill in the table.

|  | **Definition** | **Different from *journey* because…** |
|---|---|---|
| **a.** journey |  |  |
| **b.** trip |  |  |
| **c.** expedition |  |  |
| **d.** tour |  |  |

**2.** Link the words to the correct definitions.

| preposition | a group of words that form a unit within a sentence, often without a verb |
|---|---|
| phrase | a phrase with a preposition and its object |
| prepositional phrase | used with a noun or pronoun to show how things are related, e.g. place, position or time |

**3.** The poem 'In the wake of the *Fram*' contains the line: We're not the first here, but hear this first. What language device is being used?

.................................................................................................................................

.................................................................................................................................

**4. a** Underline words below that create a quiet and calm atmosphere.

Moveless fish in the water gleam

By silver reeds in a silver stream.

**b** Explain your answer.

.................................................................................................................................

.................................................................................................................................

.................................................................................................................................

.................................................................................................................................

.................................................................................................................................

.................................................................................................................................

## Conducting interviews

Imagine you host a breakfast programme for a local radio station. Every day you interview someone. You finish by asking them to choose a piece of their favourite music.

You are looking for your next guest to interview. The person could speak to you as themselves or pretend to be someone else.

Plan who you will interview. For example, you may choose:

- a friend to interview about hobbies or a recent achievement, such as in sports
- someone pretending to be a teacher or a police officer
- a musician who has just performed for the first time.

Before you start the interview, write notes on four questions you plan to ask before the person's favourite piece of music is requested. These notes will act as a reminder. If you listen carefully, you may be able to ask other questions that arise from something the person says.

Interviews on radio sound like conversations. Interviewers don't usually just say, for example, "What's your favourite hobby?" Instead an interviewer might say something like, "I've heard that you are a very keen long distance runner and that you practise several times a week. Doesn't that take a lot of your spare time?"

**1.** ............................................................................................................

............................................................................................................

**2.** ............................................................................................................

............................................................................................................

**3.** ............................................................................................................

............................................................................................................

**4.** ............................................................................................................

............................................................................................................

Remember you have an audience to entertain. So how will you introduce your interview and how will you finish it?

The introduction: ..............................................................................

............................................................................................................

The end of the interview: ..................................................................

............................................................................................................

# Fiction versus non-fiction

Why do some people choose to read fiction and others devote their reading time to non-fiction? Which do you prefer?

Write a short essay considering:

- reasons why people enjoy reading fiction
- reasons why people choose to read non-fiction
- which you prefer and why
- what you would choose to read on holiday.

Paragraph 1 – reasons why people enjoy reading fiction

.........................................................................................................................................

.........................................................................................................................................

.........................................................................................................................................

.........................................................................................................................................

.........................................................................................................................................

Paragraph 2 – reasons why people choose to read non-fiction

.........................................................................................................................................

.........................................................................................................................................

.........................................................................................................................................

.........................................................................................................................................

.........................................................................................................................................

Paragraph 3 – which you prefer reading and why, and the titles of books, articles or websites you would read on holiday

.........................................................................................................................................

.........................................................................................................................................

.........................................................................................................................................

.........................................................................................................................................

.........................................................................................................................................

## Crazy paragraphs

The eight sentences on this page make one paragraph, but they are in the wrong order.

Decide on the right order and write the paragraph below.

.................................................................................

.................................................................................

.................................................................................

.................................................................................

.................................................................................

.................................................................................

.................................................................................

.................................................................................

.................................................................................

.................................................................................

.................................................................................

.................................................................................

.................................................................................

.................................................................................

.................................................................................

.................................................................................

.................................................................................

I had overslept so there was absolutely no time for my daily shower.

With a sinking feeling, I realised I'd be late for work.

It was already 8.40 a.m.

It was eight o'clock!

Yesterday I woke up from a long sleep and looked at my watch.

Of course it wouldn't start and therefore I'd have to catch a bus.

I threw on my clothes and rushed downstairs.

Grabbing a piece of bread, I rushed to my car.

## Dragonland

Dragons exist in the myths of nations all over the world. Heroes often fought them.

**1.** Read this article about dragons.

Have you seen pictures of dragons with their long tails, which often have sharp spikes and even an arrowhead on the end? No one knows where the idea of a dragon came from, but originally the word was Greek and it meant a big snake or a water snake.

Sometime in history, artists gave dragons legs and huge, flappy wings and they started to look more like dinosaurs. Chinese and Vietnamese dragons were friendly. In China, they were associated with power and majesty, and in Vietnam a dragon brought rain. However, in most places the dragon was a savage beast with hard skin looking like armour and it had to be overcome by a hero.

Certainly, pictures of dragons, with their forked tongues and pointed teeth, are all very similar. Some artists show them flying, but this is rare. Others show them breathing fire, although not all dragons do this. Often the back of the dragon's neck, like the rest of its body, is covered with what look like very sharp spikes. Of course dragons, which live in rivers or in underground lairs, are very large creatures.

**2.** What would you expect to see in a picture of an evil dragon? List eight features.

.................................................... ....................................................

.................................................... ....................................................

.................................................... ....................................................

.................................................... ....................................................

**3.** Now use your notes to write a paragraph about the appearance of the dragon in the picture. Write in sentences and don't copy phrases from the article.

........................................................................................................

........................................................................................................

........................................................................................................

........................................................................................................

........................................................................................................

# Don't argue with me!

1. You can use discourse markers to change the direction of
   an argument. Take part in the argument below, which is set
   out like a play. Here you will be using discourse markers
   that express contrast.

   **Huang:** I think school uniform is a really good idea because I look
   really neat and tidy.

   **You:** Well, that's true. However, ................................................................

   ..............................................................................................................................

   ...................................................................................................................... .

   **Huang:** I can see your argument about some of the boys who make the
   uniform look untidy but, nevertheless, ..............................................

   ..............................................................................................................................

   ...................................................................................................................... .

   Another thing is that if everyone wears the same, it stops
   people who are rich showing off.

   **You:** Yes, but it also stops individuality. I respect your arguments,
   but in spite of what you say, ...............................................................

   ...................................................................................................................... .

2. Now here is a Principal speaking at assembly. Fill in the gaps
   in what she has to say. The discourse markers here will show
   the consequences of people's actions.

   **Principal:** Today I have good news and not so good news.
   I am very happy to report that the gymnastics team have won
   their area tournament. As a result, ....................................................
   On a less happy note, four students in the last two days have been
   reported to me for not wearing their school uniform properly.
   Consequently, ................................................................................................

   ..............................................................................................................................

   Finally, there has been far too much noise going on in the area outside
   my meeting room. You probably know that I receive many visitors and we
   need quiet to discuss matters of importance to us all. Therefore, I have
   decided ..............................................................................................................

   ...................................................................................................................... .

# 7

# Pin down the meaning

Do the following three activities. You'll need to find a partner to help you with the first two.

1.  Below are six definitions of common words. Read one definition out at a time and the other person has to guess the word. Write the words in the spaces.

    **a**  The young of some kinds of fly: ............................................................

    **b**  The molten rock that flows from a volcano: ............................................

    **c**  The adjective to describe a volcano that has not erupted for a long time: ............................................................................

    **d**  A wooden or concrete beam that the tracks of a railway rest on: ....................................................................................

    **e**  A wagon on a North American railroad: ..................................................

    **f**  A light cardboard or plastic container: ....................................................

2.  Act out each of the following words. Your partner has to guess what they are.

    | | | |
    |---|---|---|
    | dice | statue | oblong |
    | handkerchief | playing any musical instrument | feeling nervous |

3.  Come up with a definition for each of the following words and write it in the space.

    **a**  errand: .......................................................................................................

    **b**  equator: ....................................................................................................

    **c**  escalator: ..................................................................................................

    **d**  eruption: ...................................................................................................

    **e**  estuary: .....................................................................................................

    **f**  eternal: ......................................................................................................

4.  Compare each of your definitions in question **3a–f** with one from a dictionary. Which was better?

# Writing an alternative ending

Read your story about a superhero again, looking in particular at the last two paragraphs. There is a turning point when things probably get better for the superhero. Then there is an exciting climax and the ending follows.

Imagine things had turned out very differently. Write a new version of paragraphs 4 and 5. If it was a happy story before, make it tragic now, or the other way round. The words you choose will help to change the atmosphere of the story, perhaps from joy to sadness.

.................................................................................................................................................................

.................................................................................................................................................................

.................................................................................................................................................................

.................................................................................................................................................................

.................................................................................................................................................................

.................................................................................................................................................................

.................................................................................................................................................................

.................................................................................................................................................................

.................................................................................................................................................................

.................................................................................................................................................................

.................................................................................................................................................................

.................................................................................................................................................................

.................................................................................................................................................................

.................................................................................................................................................................

.................................................................................................................................................................

.................................................................................................................................................................

.................................................................................................................................................................

.................................................................................................................................................................

.................................................................................................................................................................

.................................................................................................................................................................

.................................................................................................................................................................

# Heroic history quiz

1. For many years people believed the Amazons were fictional characters from mythology. Who changed this view and what was the evidence that supported their claim?

   ......................................................................................................

   ......................................................................................................

2. Write a sentence that links these three words: *legend*, *tradition* and *fiction*.

   ......................................................................................................

3. 'My little sister let out a howl like a wounded animal because I told her not to eat any more chocolate.' What term do we use for 'like a wounded animal' and what does it tell you about the girl's howl?

   ......................................................................................................

4. Choose the correct definition. Discourse markers are:

   ☐ words that are always adjectives     ☐ words and phrases that show the direction of an argument

   ☐ arguments that are for and against an issue     ☐ the first sentence in a paragraph.

5. Explain what is meant by a turning point in a story.

   ......................................................................................................

6. Solve these anagrams for words that mean ways of talking together.

   a   Aunt Germ: ......................................................................................

   b   Overcoats Inn: ...............................................................................

   c   Eat bed: .........................................................................................

7. An octogenarian is 79 years old – true or false? Give a reason for your answer.

   ......................................................................................................

8. The most exciting part of a story that I write should be:

   ☐ at the beginning     ☐ in the last sentence

   ☐ in the second paragraph     ☐ near the end of the story.

## My favourite book

_____'s favourite book

Illustration of my favourite book

Name of favourite book

........................................................................

Author(s)

........................................................................

**Book summary**

........................................................................

........................................................................

........................................................................

........................................................................

Reasons why this is my favourite book

_Identify techniques used by the author where possible._

........................................................................

........................................................................

........................................................................

........................................................................

Favourite character (with explanation)

........................................................................

........................................................................

........................................................................

# A writer's craft

1. Writers use a range of techniques to keep the reader engaged. Fill in each gap below using the correct technique from the cloud.

   **a** Setting the ........................................ for each new segment

   **b** Developing the ........................................ of the key people

   **c** Using ........................................ language

   **d** Providing a ........................................ to the story

   **e** Including ........................................ between the main characters

   **f** Dropping ........................................ about what might happen next

   **g** Holding back ........................................ to make the reader curious

   **h** Addressing the reader using a specific ........................................ voice

   **i** Including a ........................................ to confuse or distract the reader

   > descriptive   hints   background
   > red herring   narrative   scene
   > characterisation
   > dialogue   information

2. Writers have a clear purpose in mind when writing. Give one specific purpose for each of these novels (not just to entertain).

   **a** A detective story ........................................

   **b** A story set in 17th-century Malaysia ........................................

   **c** A suspense story about a creature ........................................

   **d** A dystopian tale about the future ........................................

   **e** A story about two famous athletes due to compete against each other at the Olympics ........................................

3. What is your favourite novel? Think about its purpose and the main techniques it uses to keep the reader engaged.

   **a** My favourite book of all time is ........................................

   **b** The main three techniques it uses are:

   - ........................................   • ........................................   • ........................................

4. Now think about writing your own novel.

   My setting ........................................

   My main characters ........................................

   My purpose to engage the reader ........................................

   How will it end? ........................................

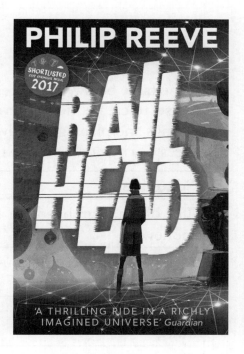

PHILIP REEVE

SHORTLISTED 2017

RAIL HEAD

'A THRILLING RIDE IN A RICHLY IMAGINED UNIVERSE' *Guardian*

## Using adverbs and adverbials

1. Complete the adjective and adverb chart below. The blank lines at the end are for you to insert your own suggestions.

| Adjective | Adverb |
|-----------|--------|
| rude | |
| | thoroughly |
| early | |
| actual | |
| | lazily |
| | well |
| | |
| | |
| | |

2. In the table below, pair up each sentence with an adverbial phrase, to create more interesting sentences. Try different pairings and placing the adverbial phrase in different places. Write down your extended sentences.

| Sentence | Adverbial phrase |
|----------|------------------|
| The old man grabbed the money. | after dinner |
| Mrs Lee made scrumptious cake. | with a wicked grin |
| A small mouse scuttled away. | in the street |
| The parrot flew away. | as quickly as possible |
| They decided to check the cellar again. | for her children |

....................................................................

....................................................................

....................................................................

....................................................................

## Drama

Think of a scene from a book you have read. Rewrite it as a scene from a play, TV show or film. Continue the scene in any way you wish. Remember to set out your script correctly, with:

- the name of the character speaking in the margin

- stage or film directions in brackets, written in the present tense.

# Relative pronouns

1. Complete the following sentences by adding the correct relative pronouns.

   a  The woman ................................. lives next door looks quite scary.

   b  I love the cake ................................. you made today.

   c  Danni, ................................. is a swimming champion, is scared of fish!

   d  Farrah, ................................. son is travelling the world, is a teacher at our school.

   e  The huge beast ................................. was towering over us was a rhinoceros.

   f  A police officer, ................................. car was parked nearby, spotted the thief.

2. Write three sentences using different relative pronouns. In each case, identify the relative pronoun by circling or underlining it.

.............................................................................................................

.............................................................................................................

.............................................................................................................

.............................................................................................................

.............................................................................................................

.............................................................................................................

.............................................................................................................

.............................................................................................................

.............................................................................................................

.............................................................................................................

.............................................................................................................

.............................................................................................................

.............................................................................................................

.............................................................................................................

# Show and tell

Explain what techniques the writer uses in each of these extracts to create an impression of character.

### Extract 1

1     He was a tall man, as thin as a noodle and with a face that was so sallow it was just about the same colour. His grey-white hair – what there was of it – waved and wandered all over the sides of his head. Flecks of black here and there in his hair made
5     it look as if black pepper had been sprinkled liberally onto a mound of salt.

**From *Thief* by Malorie Blackman**

..................................................................................................................................................................

..................................................................................................................................................................

..................................................................................................................................................................

..................................................................................................................................................................

### Extract 2

1     Jim Jarvis. Want to know who that is? It's me! That's my name. Only thing I've got, is my name. And I've given it away to this man. Barnie, his name is, or something like that. He told me once, only I forgot it, see, and I don't like to ask him again.
5     'Mister', I call him, to his face, that is. But there's a little space in my head where his name is Barnie. He keeps asking me things. He wants to know my story, that's what he tells me. My story, mister? What d'you want to know that for? Ain't much of a story, mine ain't.

**From *Street Child* by Berlie Doherty**

..................................................................................................................................................................

..................................................................................................................................................................

..................................................................................................................................................................

..................................................................................................................................................................

..................................................................................................................................................................

## Very short stories

People may not realise it, but tweets are simply stories with a 140-character limit. For example:

> Mum was baking cinnamon cookies in the kitchen. She knows I hate cinnamon. When she turned round, I noticed her eyes were the wrong colour...

Some stories are even shorter and can be expressed in six words:

> My stomach hurts. It is lunchtime.

These types of very short stories are sometimes called flash fiction.

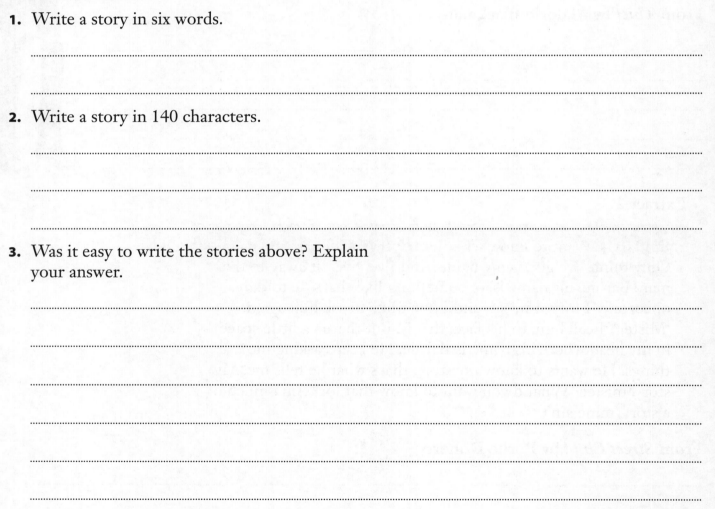

**1.** Write a story in six words.

......................................................................................................................

......................................................................................................................

**2.** Write a story in 140 characters.

......................................................................................................................

......................................................................................................................

......................................................................................................................

**3.** Was it easy to write the stories above? Explain your answer.

......................................................................................................................

......................................................................................................................

......................................................................................................................

......................................................................................................................

......................................................................................................................

# 8

# Exciting escapades quiz

**1.** Name two techniques that writers use in the openings of
books or stories to engage the reader.

...................................................................................................................

...................................................................................................................

**2.** State one way in which you can turn an adjective into
an adverb.

...................................................................................................................

**3.** Give two examples of adverbs.

...................................................................................................................

**4.** Name three techniques that writers use to convey
character.

...................................................................................................................

...................................................................................................................

...................................................................................................................

**5.** List some of the vocabulary used to discuss books and
stories.

...................................................................................................................

...................................................................................................................

...................................................................................................................

**6.** When do you use *who*, *which* or *that* in relative clauses? Use
examples to support your answer.

...................................................................................................................

...................................................................................................................

...................................................................................................................

**7.** What is flash fiction?

...................................................................................................................

...................................................................................................................

## Soap-box oratory

People who wanted to make speeches in public used to stand on tough crates used for transporting soap. Audiences would assemble round them and join in.

Here's your opportunity to have a say about whatever you feel strongly about.

1.  Start with some practice. Stand on your box in a marketplace and persuade passers-by to buy something. Make your fruit juicy and cheap, or make your kitchen utensil solve everyone's problems! You'll need a loud voice.

    Item for sale is: ....................................................................................

    ....................................................................................................................

    Three ways of persuading passers-by to buy it:

    ● .............................................................................................................

    .................................................................................................................

    ● .............................................................................................................

    .................................................................................................................

    ● .............................................................................................................

    .................................................................................................................

2.  Now choose a pet subject – something you think ought to be done or ought not to be done; something you dislike and think ought to be banned; something that probably few people will agree about.

    My pet subject is ...................................................................................

    Three reasons why my audience should agree with me and do something about it:

    ● .............................................................................................................

    .................................................................................................................

    ● .............................................................................................................

    .................................................................................................................

    ● .............................................................................................................

    .................................................................................................................

# More interesting prefixes

1. How many words can you think of that begin with *trans-*, meaning 'across?

.....................................................................................................................................

.....................................................................................................................................

2. *Cata* means 'down' in Greek. Find four words in your dictionary that seem to fit this meaning.

a ...................................................................   c ...................................................................

b ...................................................................   d ...................................................................

3. *Tele* means 'far off'. Write sentences to show you know the meanings of these words.

a Telescope: ..............................................................................................

.....................................................................................................................................

b Telecommunications: ...........................................................................

.....................................................................................................................................

c Telepathy: ...............................................................................................

.....................................................................................................................................

4. In the diagram opposite, you will find a mixture of words with *contra-* (against), *hos-* (a place where guests are received) and *voc-* (to call or summon). Look up the precise meaning of each word in a dictionary and write them out below.

hostel | hospice
vocalist | vocation
hospital | contraflow
contradict | contraband
vociferous | hospitality

........................................................................................

........................................................................................

........................................................................................

........................................................................................

........................................................................................

........................................................................................

## The long and the short of it

Can you write a short short story in 75 words? One extra
thing – you must include at least one short sentence for
effect. It can be an ordinary sentence or an exclamation or
rhetorical question. Simple.

Here's an example:

> Giorgio woke with a start. He crept to the window just as an
> enormous gust of wind blew the curtain in his face, and what he saw
> filled him with fear. Emerging from the trees was a monster with
> terrible jaws, growling as it approached the house. What was it?
> Giorgio stood rooted to the spot as the monster came nearer, raising
> its paw, threatening, roaring, a nightmare. Giorgio woke with a start.

Now write your story below. When you have finished, share
your story with other students and see who has made the best,
complete one.

.................................................................................................................................

.................................................................................................................................

.................................................................................................................................

.................................................................................................................................

.................................................................................................................................

.................................................................................................................................

.................................................................................................................................

.................................................................................................................................

.................................................................................................................................

.................................................................................................................................

.................................................................................................................................

.................................................................................................................................

.................................................................................................................................

.................................................................................................................................

# 9

## I don't agree with you

Here is a chance for you to reply with your own opinion.

You have just read on an Internet blog that Radio Man Sam objects to young people watching TV. He wants them to spend less time staring at TV screens and more time listening to radio and podcasts at home and more time outside. Radio Man Sam worries about the effects on children's mental health of pointless comedies and police dramas. He is also concerned about the impact of hundreds of commercial adverts that appear so randomly.

Reply to his blog post.

Radio Man Sam has a point, but I ..............................................................................................................

..................................................................................................................................................................................

..................................................................................................................................................................................

..................................................................................................................................................................................

..................................................................................................................................................................................

..................................................................................................................................................................................

..................................................................................................................................................................................

..................................................................................................................................................................................

..................................................................................................................................................................................

..................................................................................................................................................................................

..................................................................................................................................................................................

..................................................................................................................................................................................

..................................................................................................................................................................................

..................................................................................................................................................................................

..................................................................................................................................................................................

..................................................................................................................................................................................

..................................................................................................................................................................................

..................................................................................................................................................................................

..................................................................................................................................................................................

## Who, which and whose

1. Look at this paragraph. It has too many short sentences.

   This is Mr Alioke. He is my uncle. He is a very rich man and he owns the Alioke estate. It is a major pineapple-producing complex. He is also a very wise man. His opinion is one I greatly respect.

   Rewrite this paragraph in three sentences. Use each of *who*, *which* and *whose* once.

   ........................................................................................................................................

   ........................................................................................................................................

   ........................................................................................................................................

   ........................................................................................................................................

   ........................................................................................................................................

2. Complete these sentences, using *who*, *which* or *whose*.

   **a** I threw the ball to my sister ...........................................................................

   ........................................................................................................................................

   **b** Because I had not done my homework I was afraid to face up to my teacher

   ........................................................................................................................................

   **c** I just missed the bus ...................................................................................................

   **d** I picked up the kitten ..................................................................................................

   **e** ........................................................................................................................................

   ........................... brothers and sisters had arranged a surprise party that afternoon.

3. Make up your own sentences using:

   Who: ..............................................................................................................................

   ........................................................................................................................................

   Which: ...........................................................................................................................

   ........................................................................................................................................

   Whose: ...........................................................................................................................

   ........................................................................................................................................

   ........................................................................................................................................

# All about my school

Discuss how you would make a 15-minute podcast about your school.

**1.** Make a list of things you would want to include.

- ....................................................................................................
- ....................................................................................................
- ....................................................................................................
- ....................................................................................................
- ....................................................................................................

**2.** Who would you interview?

- ....................................................................................................
- ....................................................................................................
- ....................................................................................................

**3.** How would you begin? Write the first few lines of your introduction.

....................................................................................................

....................................................................................................

....................................................................................................

....................................................................................................

....................................................................................................

....................................................................................................

**4.** Discuss what camera shots you would want to use for the different sections.

**5.** Role-play the interviews and coverage of the different aspects of school life you will cover, such as:

- a sports team
- school uniform
- the dining hall.

## Checking your work

Whenever you write for an audience of any kind, whether it's for your friends in a text, for your teachers in essays or in an article for a school magazine, it's important that you check carefully that you have written what you meant to.

For example, simply using a negative when you meant to use a positive can change the whole meaning, as in this sentence where a teenager thinks he is agreeing to meet his friend the next day:

Of course I can't meet you at the Internet cafe tomorrow.

Read this opening paragraph from a blog on how the Internet has changed people's lives and write the correct version below, without any mistakes. The writer has made mistakes with spelling, punctuation and grammar.

Can u imagin a world with the Internet. How did we all suvive when we neded to look up somthin or chat to a frend about a important issue. Familyswouldnt have been able two communicate if there relatives were on the other side of world and them doing busness would have to wait for letters to be posted and arrive days latter. Nowdays with instant messaging group calls an instant comunication everyone can benefit. Personally, Ifi want too find out information on a topic I know noting about, I just type in a serchreqest and Im ready to begin my work. it is so easy anyone can't do it? Even my grandmother who is eightyfour has her own webpaige and over a thousand followers on a poplar chat engin. Shes even more fame than me!

## Corrected version

.......................................................................................................................

.......................................................................................................................

.......................................................................................................................

.......................................................................................................................

.......................................................................................................................

.......................................................................................................................

.......................................................................................................................

.......................................................................................................................

.......................................................................................................................

# Digital diversity quiz

**1. a** Why is speaking in public sometimes called soap-box oratory?

.................................................................................................................

**b** What opportunities does it give a speaker?

.................................................................................................................

**2. a** What have *catastrophe* and *downfall* in common?

.................................................................................................................

**b** What have a hotel and a hospital in common?

.................................................................................................................

**3.** The speaker on the soap-box said, "We're all getting wet, I know. But who cares? We're here for a very important reason." Why was his question rhetorical?

.................................................................................................................

**4.** What would you say to these students if you were a teacher?

**a** I always write in long sentences to sound clever.

.................................................................................................................

**b** I always write in short sentences to make them easy to read.

.................................................................................................................

**5.** When you wrote your newspaper or magazine article, what did you have to remember about your language, and why?

.................................................................................................................

**6.** Fill in the gap below. What part of speech did you use?

This is the man ....................... dog ran into my garden.

**7.** When you check your work, what sort of mistakes are you looking for?

.................................................................................................................

**8.** Explain the confusion between *quite* and *quiet*, and *their* and *there*.

.................................................................................................................

.................................................................................................................

# Language and literacy reference

**Active voice versus passive voice** – Verbs are active when the subject of the sentence (the agent) does the action. Example: *The shark swallowed the fish*. Active verbs are used more in informal speech or writing.

Verbs are passive when the subject of the sentence has the action done to it. Example: *The fish was swallowed by the shark*. Passive verbs are used in more formal writing such as reports. Examples: *An eye-witness was interviewed by the police. Results have been analysed by the sales team*.

Sometimes turning an active sentence to passive, or vice versa, simply means moving the agent:

- The shark (agent and subject) + verb = active
- The fish (object) + verb = passive

**Adjective** – An adjective describes a noun or adds to its meaning. They are usually found in front of a noun. Example: *Green emeralds and glittering diamonds*. Adjectives can also come after a verb. Examples: *It was big. They looked hungry*. Sometimes you can use two adjectives together. Example: *tall and handsome*. This is called an adjectival phrase.

Adjectives can be used to describe degrees of intensity. To make a comparative adjective you usually add *–er* (or use *more*). Examples: *quicker; more beautiful*. To make a superlative you add *–est* (or use *most*). Examples: *quickest; most beautiful*.

**Adverb** – An adverb adds further meaning to a verb. Many are formed by adding *-ly* to an adjective. Example: *slow/slowly*. They often come next to the verb in a sentence. Adverbs can tell the reader: how – *quickly, stupidly, amazingly*; where – *there, here, everywhere*; when – *yesterday, today, now*; how often – *occasionally, often*.

**Adverbial phrase** – The part of a sentence that tells the reader when, where or how something happens is called an adverbial phrase. It is a group of words that functions as an adverb.

Examples: *I'm going to the dentist <u>tomorrow morning</u>* (when). *The teacher spoke to us <u>as if he was in</u> a bad mood* (how); *Sam ran <u>all the way home</u>* (where). These adverbials are called adverbials of time, manner and place.

**Alliteration** – Alliteration occurs when two or more nearby words start with the same sound. Example: *A slow, sad, sorrowful song*.

**Antecedent** – An antecedent is the person or thing that a pronoun refers back to. Example: *President Alkira realised that his life was in danger*. 'President Alkira' is the antecedent here.

**Antonym** – An antonym is a word or phrase that means the opposite of another word or phrase in the same language. Example: *shut* is an antonym of *open*. Synonyms and antonyms can be used to add variation and depth to your writing.

**Audience** – The readers of a text and/or the people for whom the author is writing; the term can also apply to those who watch a film or to television viewers.

**Clause** – A clause is a group of words that contains a subject and a verb. Example: *I ran*. In this clause, *I* is the subject and *ran* is the verb.

**Cliché** – An expression, idiom or phrase that has been repeated so often it has lost its significance.

**Colloquial language** – Informal, everyday speech as used in conversation; it may include slang expressions. Not appropriate in written reports, essays or exams.

**Colon** – A colon is a punctuation mark (:) used to indicate that an example, explanation or list is being used by the writer within the sentence. Examples: *You will need: a notebook, a pencil, a notepad and a ruler. I am quick at running: as fast as a cheetah*.

**Conditional tense** – This tense is used to talk about something that might happen. Conditionals are sometimes called 'if' clauses. They can be used to talk about imaginary situations or possible real-life scenarios. Examples: *If it gets any colder the river will freeze. If I had a million pounds I would buy a zoo.*

**Conjugate** – To change the tense or subject of a verb.

**Conjunction** – A conjunction is a word used to link clauses within a sentence such as: *and, but, so, until, when, as*. Example: *He had a book in his hand when he stood up.*

**Connectives** – A connective is a word or a phrase that links clauses or sentences. Connectives can be conjunctions. Examples: *but, when, because*. Connectives can also be connecting adverbs. Examples: *then, therefore, finally*.

**Continuous tense** – This tense is used to tell you that something is continuing to happen. Example: *I am watching football.*

**Discourse markers** – Words and phrases such as *on the other hand, to sum up, however* and *therefore* are called discourse markers because they mark stages along an argument. Using them will make your paragraphs clearer and more orderly.

**Exclamation** – An exclamation shows someone's feelings about something. Example: *What a pity!*

**Exclamation mark** – An exclamation mark makes a phrase or a short sentence stand out. You usually use it in phrases like 'How silly I am!' and more freely in dialogue when people are speaking. Don't use it at the end of a long, factual sentence and don't use it too often.

**Idiom** – An idiom is a colourful expression which has become fixed in the language. It is a phrase which has a meaning that cannot be worked out from the meanings of the words in it. Examples: *in hot water* means 'in trouble'; *It's raining cats and dogs* means 'it's raining heavily'.

**Imagery** – A picture in words, often using a metaphor or simile (figurative language) which describes something in detail: writers use visual, aural (auditory) or tactile imagery to convey how something looks, sounds or feels in all forms of writing, not just fiction or poetry. Imagery helps the reader to feel like they are actually there.

**Irregular verb** – An irregular verb does not follow the standard grammatical rules. Each has to be learned as it does not follow any pattern. For example, *catch* becomes *caught* in the past tense, not *catched*.

**Metaphor** – A metaphor is a figure of speech in which one thing is actually said to be the other. Example: *This man is a lion in battle.*

**Non-restrictive clause** – A non-restrictive clause provides additional information about a noun. They can be taken away from the sentence and it will still make sense. They are separated from the rest of the sentence by commas (or brackets). Example: *The principal, who liked order, was shocked and angry.*

**Onomatopoeia** – Words that imitate sounds, sensations or textures. Examples: *bang, crash, prickly, squishy.*

**Paragraph** – A group of sentences (minimum of two, except in modern fiction) linked by a single idea or subject. Each paragraph should contain a topic sentence. Paragraphs should be planned, linked and organised to lead up to a conclusion in most forms of writing.

**Parenthetical phrase** – A parenthetical phrase is a phrase that has been added into a sentence which is already complete, to provide additional information. It is usually separated from other clauses using a pair of commas, dashes or brackets (parentheses). Examples: *The leading goal scorer at the 2018 World Cup – Harry Kane, playing for England – scored six goals. The leading actor in the film, Hollywood great Gene Kelly, is captivating.*

**Passive voice** – See active voice.

**Person (first, second or third)** – The first person is used to talk about oneself – *I/we*. The second person is used to address the person who is listening or reading – *you*. The third person is used to refer to someone else – *he, she, it, they*.

- *I feel like I've been here for days*. (first person)
- *Look what you get when you join the club*. (second person)
- *He says it takes real courage*. (third person)

**Personification** – Personification can work at two levels: it can give an animal the characteristics of a human and it can give an abstract thing the characteristics of a human or an animal. Example: *I was looking Death in the face*.

**Prefix** – A prefix is an element placed at the beginning of a word to modify its meaning. Prefixes include: *dis-, un-, im-, in-, il-, ir-*. Examples: *impossible, inconvenient, irresponsible*.

**Preposition** – A preposition is a word that indicates place (*on, in*), direction (*over, beyond*) or time (*during, on*) among others.

**Pronoun** – A pronoun is a word that can replace a noun, often to avoid repetition. Example: *I put the book on the table. It was next to the plant*. 'It' refers back to the book in the first sentence.

- Subject pronouns act as the subject of the sentence: *I, you, he, she, it*.
- Object pronouns act as the object of the sentence: *me, you, him, her, it, us, you, them*.
- Possessive pronouns show that something belongs to someone: *mine, yours, his, hers, its, ours, yours, theirs*.
- Demonstrative pronouns refer to things: *this, that, those, these*.

**Questions** – There are different types of questions.

- Closed questions – This type of question can be answered with a single-word response, can be answered with 'yes' or 'no', can be answered by choosing from a list of possible answers, and identifies a piece of specific information.

- Open questions – This type of question cannot be answered with a single-word response; it requires a more thoughtful answer than just 'yes' or 'no'.

- Leading questions – This type of question suggests what answer should be given. Example: *Why are robot servants bad for humans?* This suggests to the responder that robots are bad as the question is "why are they bad?" rather than "do you think they are bad?" Also called loaded questions.

- Rhetorical question – Rhetorical questions are questions that do not require an answer but serve to give the speaker an excuse to explain his/her views. Rhetorical questions should be avoided in formal writing and essays. Example: *Who wouldn't want to go on holiday?*

**Register** – The appropriate style and tone of language chosen for a specific purpose and/or audience. When speaking to your friends and family you use an informal register whereas you use a more formal tone if talking to someone older, in a position of authority or who you do not know very well. Examples: *I'm going to do up the new place*. (informal) *I am planning to decorate my new flat*. (more formal)

**Regular verb** – A regular verb follows the rules when conjugated (e.g. by adding *–ed* in the past tense, such as *walk* which becomes *walked*).

**Relative clause** – Relative clauses are a type of subordinate clause. They describe or explain something that has just been mentioned using *who, whose, which, where, whom, that* or *when*. Example: *The girl who was standing next to the counter was carrying a small dog*.

**Relative pronoun** – A relative pronoun does what it says – it takes an idea and relates it to a person or a thing. Be careful to use *who* for people and *which* for things. Examples: *I talked to your teacher, who told me about your unfinished homework. This is my favourite photo, which shows you the beach and the palm trees*.

**Restrictive clause** – Restrictive clauses identify the person or thing that is being referred to and are vital to the meaning of the sentence. They are not separated from the rest of the sentence by a comma. With restrictive clauses, you can often drop the relative pronoun. Example: *The letter [that] I wrote yesterday was lost.*

**Semi-colon** – A semi-colon is a punctuation mark (;) that separates two main clauses. It is stronger than a comma but not as strong as a full stop. Each clause could form a sentence by itself. Example: *I like cheese; it is delicious.*

**Sentence** – A sentence is a group of words that expresses a complete thought. All sentences begin with a capital letter and end with a full stop, question mark or exclamation mark.

- Simple sentences are made up of one clause. Example: *I am hungry.*

- Complex sentences are made up of one main clause and one, or more, subordinate clauses. A subordinate clause cannot stand on its own and relies on the main clause. Example: *When I joined the drama club, I did not know that it was going to be so much fun.*

- Compound sentences are made up of two or more main clauses, usually joined by a conjunction. Example: *I am hungry and I am thirsty.*

Good writers use sentences of different lengths to vary the pace of their writing. Short sentences can make a strong impact while longer sentences can make text flow.

**Simile** – A simile is a figure of speech in which two things are compared using the linking words *like* or *as*. Example: *In battle, he was as brave as a lion.*

**Simple past tense** – This tense is used to tell you that something happened in the past. Only one verb is required. Example: *I wore a hat.*

**Simple present tense** – This tense is used to tell you that something is happening now. Only one verb is required. Example: *I wear a hat.*

**Standard English** – Standard English is the form of English used in most writing and by educated speakers. It can be spoken with any accent. There are many slight differences between Standard English and local ways of speaking. Example: *We were robbed* is Standard English but in speech some people say, *We was robbed.*

**Suffix** – A suffix is an element placed at the end of a word to modify its meaning. Suffixes include: *-ible, -able, -ful, -less*. Examples: *useful, useless, meaningful, meaningless.*

**Summary** – A summary is a record of the main points of something you have read, seen or heard. Keep to the point and keep it short. Use your own words to make everything clear.

**Synonym** – A synonym is a word or phrase that means nearly the same as another word or phrase in the same language. Example: *shut* is a synonym of *close*. Synonyms and antonyms can be used to add variation and depth to your writing.

**Syntax** – The study of how words are organised in a sentence.

**Tense** – A tense is a verb form that shows whether events happen in the past, present or the future.

- *The Pyramids are on the west bank of the River Nile.* (present tense)

- *They were built as enormous tombs.* (past tense)

- *They will stand for centuries to come.* (future tense)

Most verbs change their spelling by adding *–ed* to form the past tense. Example: *walk/walked.* Some have irregular spellings. Example: *catch/caught.*

**Topic sentence** – The key sentence of a paragraph that contains the principal idea or subject being discussed.

# Word cloud dictionary

**Word and definition**

**24/7** *adverb*
Twenty-four hours a day, seven days a week; all the time.

**Allegedly** *adverb*
Claimed to be the case but without proof.

**Ambush** *verb*
To lie in wait for someone in order to attack them.

**Ancient** *adjective*
Belonging to the distant past; very old.

**Apocalypse** *noun*
The complete final destruction of the world, as described in the biblical book of Revelation.

**Array** *noun*
An ordered series or arrangement.

**Are you dissing…?**
An informal expression that means 'are you speaking disrespectfully or criticising…?'

**Artery** *noun*
Walled tube through which blood is conveyed from the heart to the body.

**Astonishingly** *adverb*
Extremely, surprisingly or impressively.

**Atom** *noun*
The smallest particle of a chemical element.

**Awful** *adjective*
Very bad.

**Boom** *noun*
A loud, deep sound that resonates strongly like a gong.

**Booming** *adjective*
Very loud.

**Burst** *verb*
To rush suddenly and uncontrollably.

**Calamity** *noun*
An event that causes great damage or distress.

**Calcium** *noun*
A chemical substance found in teeth, bones, and lime.

**Carbohydrate** *noun*
A compound of carbon, oxygen, and hydrogen (e.g. sugar or starch) found in food and a source of energy.

**Cataclysm** *noun*
A violent upheaval or disaster.

**Catastrophe** *noun*
A sudden great disaster.

**Notes**

| Word and definition | Notes |
|---|---|

**Cavernous** *adjective*
A cavernous room or space is a huge empty one.

**Cereal** *noun*
A grass producing seeds which are used as food, e.g. wheat, barley, or rice; a breakfast food made from these seeds.

**Character** *noun*
A person appearing in a story, film, or play.

**Classical** *adjective*
To do with ancient Greek or Roman literature or art; classical art or music is serious or conventional in style, and is often associated with the 18th century in Europe.

**Cliff-hanger** *noun*
A tense and exciting ending to an episode of a story.

**Clump** *noun*
A cluster or mass of things or people.

**Colossal** *adjective*
Extremely large; enormous.

**Communicate** *verb*
To share or exchange information, news or ideas.

**Compatible** *adjective*
Able to exist together without problems.

**Concoction** *noun*
A mixture of various ingredients or elements.

**Confusedly heaped** *adverb + verb*
Lying in a disorganised pile.

**Contribute** *verb*
To give views in a discussion.

**Creative** *adjective*
Showing imagination and thought as well as skill.

**Crescent** *noun*
A narrow curved shape coming to a point at each end.

**Debacle** *noun*
A complete failure or disaster.

**Deep** *adjective*
Going a long way down or back or in.

**Destroy** *verb*
To damage something so badly that it is completely spoiled.

**Diet** *noun*
The sort of foods usually eaten by a person or animal; special meals that a person eats in order to be healthy or to reduce weight.

**Discontented** *adjective*
Noun *discontent*, lack of contentment; dissatisfaction.

**Word and definition**

**Discover** *verb*
To become aware of.

**Doubt** *verb*
To feel uncertain about something.

**Doze** *verb*
To be lightly asleep.

**Drapery** *noun*
Cloth arranged in loose folds.

**Dude** *noun*
A person; a man.

**Eco-magazine** *noun*
An environmentally friendly collection of articles.

**Elliptical** *adjective*
Shaped like an ellipse.

**Enduring** *adjective*
Verb *to endure*, to suffer or put up with difficulty or pain; to continue to exist, to last.

**Engage** *verb*
To engage someone's interest or attention is to attract and retain their attention.

**Extraordinary** *adjective*
Very unusual or strange.

**Fantasy** *noun*
An imaginative piece of music or writing.

**Fat** *noun*
A white greasy substance found in animal bodies and certain seeds; oil or grease used in cooking.

**Fiasco** *noun*
A humiliating or embarrassing failure.

**Flicker** *verb*
To shine unsteadily; to make small, quick movements.

**Flood** *verb*
To arrive in overwhelming amounts or quantities.

**Fringe** *noun*
A decorative edging with many threads hanging down loosely.

**Gateway** *noun*
An opening containing a gate; a frame or arch built over a gate.

**Gawk** *verb*
To stare openly and stupidly.

**Generate** *verb*
To produce or create.

**Glance** *verb*
To look at something briefly.

**Notes**

| Word and definition | Notes |
| --- | --- |

**Glare** *verb*
To stare angrily or fiercely; to shine with a bright or dazzling light.

**Glassy** *adjective*
Noun *glass*, a hard brittle substance that is usually transparent or translucent; a container for drinking from, made of glass; a mirror; a lens or optical instrument.

**Grind** *verb*
To crush something into tiny pieces or powder; to sharpen or smooth something by rubbing it on a rough surface.

**Grip** *verb*
to hold fir.

**Harmony** *noun*
A pleasant combination of musical notes.

**Hem** *verb*
To hem someone in is to surround them and prevent them from leaving.

**Hold your horses**
An expression that means 'wait a moment'.

**Hollow** *adjective*
Having an empty space inside, not solid.

**Huff** *noun*
The blowing out of air, as in minor or petty annoyance.

**Iconic** *adjective*
Very famous or popular; widely recognised and well-established.

**Imagination** *noun*
The ability to imagine things; the ability to be creative or inventive.

**Immune response** *noun*
Reaction of the cells and fluids of the body to a substance in the body which is not part of the body.

**Inadequacy** *noun*
A lack of the quantity or quality required.

**Incredible** *adjective*
Impossible to believe; extremely good.

**Indecision** *noun*
The inability to make decisions; hesitation.

**Insane** *adjective*
Shocking or outrageous (informal use).

**Inspiration** *noun*
A sudden brilliant idea; a person or thing that fills you with ideas or enthusiasm.

**Intimidate** *verb*
To frighten someone with threats into doing something.

**Intonation** *noun*
The tone or pitch of the voice in speaking; intoning.

**Word and definition**

**Notes**

**Itch** *verb*
To have a strong desire to do something.

**Kid** *noun*
A child (informal use).

**Layer** *noun*
A single thickness or coating.

**Legend** *noun*
A traditional story sometimes popularly regarded as historical but not authenticated.

**Leukaemia** *noun*
A type of cancer which affects the production and function of blood cells.

**Ludicrous** *adjective*
Foolish or unreasonable enough to appear out of place and amusing.

**Malevolent** *adjective*
Wishing to harm people.

**Multifarious** *adjective*
Of many kinds, very varied.

**Myth** *noun*
A traditional story, especially one concerning the early history of a people and typically involving supernatural beings or events.

**Nanoparticle** *noun*
An extremely tiny particle of matter measuring 1–100 nanometers.

**Nanotechnology** *noun*
The branch of technology that deals with dimensions of less than 100 nanometres.

**Nightmarish** *adjective*
Like a frightening dream.

**Not necessarily** *phrase*
(As a response) what has been said or suggested may not be true or unavoidable.

**Novel** *noun*
A story of fiction that fills a whole book.

**Nutrient** *noun*
A nourishing substance.

**Nutritious** *adjective*
Giving good nourishment.

**OK** *adverb, adjective*
All right.

## Word and definition

**Old-fashioned** *adjective*
Of the kind that was usual a long time ago, no longer fashionable.

**Online** *adjective*
Connected to the Internet by use of a computer or other similar device.

**Open** *adjective*
Allowing access, passage, or a view through an empty space; not closed or blocked.

**Opportunity** *noun*
A good chance to do a particular thing.

**Oval-shaped** *adjective*
Having a rounded and slightly elongated outline or shape like that of an egg.

**Overawe** *verb*
To overcome or inhibit someone with awe.

**Paralyse** *verb*
To cause paralysis in a person or a part of the body; to be paralysed with fear or emotion is to be so affected by it that you cannot act.

**Parameter** *noun*
A limit or boundary defining the scope of something.

**Participate** *verb*
To take part in something or have a share in it.

**Peptide** *noun*
A compound consisting of two or more amino acids linked in a chain.

**Perfect** *verb*
To make a thing completely free from faults or defects; make as good as possible.

**Perfection** *noun*
A perfect state or achievement.

**Perpetual** *adjective*
Lasting for a long time, occurring repeatedly, continual.

**Pierce** *verb*
To force through, penetrate like a sharp knife.

**Pitch** *noun*
The highness or lowness of a voice or a musical note.

**Pitted** *adjective*
Having a hollow or indentation on the surface.

**Pound** *verb*
To strike repeatedly with great force.

**Pre-blog** *adjective*
Before blogging.

## Notes ·

## Word and definition

**Notes**

**Prestigious** *adjective*
Inspiring respect and admiration; having high status.

**Primitive** *adjective*
At an early stage of civilisation; at an early stage of development, not complicated or sophisticated.

**Prod** *verb*
To poke something or someone; to stimulate someone into action.

**Protein** *noun*
A substance that is found in all living things and is an essential part of the food of animals.

**Pull** *noun*
A steady movement with a driving force.

**Purely** *adverb*
Entirely, completely and exclusively.

**Race** *noun*
A competition to be the first to reach a particular place or to do something.

**Rack** *verb*
To cause distress to; to stretch violently.

**Rap sheet** *noun*
A report, school file; a criminal record (informal use).

**Recite** *verb*
To read out, often from memory.

**Recommend** *verb*
To put forward with approval as being suitable for a purpose.

**Re-drafting** *noun*
The act of drafting a document or text again in a different way.

**Redundant** *adjective*
No longer needed or useful; superfluous.

**Renowned** *adjective*
Famous or celebrated.

**Repertoire** *noun*
A stock of songs, plays, jokes etc. that a person or company knows and can perform.

**Rhythmically** *adverb*
In a regular pattern of beats or stresses as in a piece of speech or music; or in a regularly recurring sequence of movements or events.

**Rough-work** *verb*
To create a first draft of something.

**Rumble** *noun*
A continuous, deep and resonant sound like thunder.

| Word and definition | Notes |
|---|---|
| **Rush** *verb*<br>To go or move quickly. | |
| **Satisfy** *verb*<br>To give someone what they need or want. | |
| **Scant** *adjective*<br>Barely enough or adequate. | |
| **Scatter** *verb*<br>To throw or send things in all directions; to run or leave quickly in all directions. | |
| **Senility** *noun*<br>The condition of being senile: weak or confused and forgetful because of old age. | |
| **Sever** *verb*<br>To cut or break something off. | |
| **Shadow** *noun*<br>The dark shape that falls on a surface when something is between the surface and a light; an area of shade. | |
| **Shrink** *verb*<br>To become smaller, or to make something smaller. | |
| **Signify** *verb*<br>To mean something. | |
| **Sitch** *noun*<br>Situation (informal use). | |
| **Slack** *adjective*<br>Not pulled or held tight, loose; not busy, not working hard. | |
| **Sleep** *verb*<br>To rest with the eyes closed, the body relaxed and the mind unconscious. | |
| **Slice** *verb*<br>To cut with or as if with a sharp instrument | |
| **Slither** *verb*<br>To move or slide across a slippery surface. | |
| **Squabble** *verb*<br>To quarrel in a fairly harmless way. | |
| **Squirm** *verb*<br>To wriggle about when you feel embarrassed or awkward. | |
| **Startling** *adjective*<br>Very surprising, astonishing or remarkable. | |
| **Still** *adjective*<br>Not moving; not disturbed by wind or sounds. | |
| **Stir** *verb*<br>To move, cause to move slightly, or to excite. | |

## Word and definition

**Stout** *adjective*
Thick and strong.

**Strand** *noun*
Each of the threads or wires twisted together to form a rope, yarn or cable.

**Strap** *verb*
To fasten or bind something with a strap or straps.

**Strike** *verb*
To hit someone or something.

**Stud** *verb*
To decorate with large-headed pieces of metal (studs).

**Stuff** *noun*
Worthless material; speech, writing or ideas without much value

**Stumble** *verb*
To find or encounter by chance.

**Sunken** *adjective*
Sunk deeply into a surface.

**Supposedly** *adverb*
According to what is generally assumed or believed.

**Swishing** *adjective*
Swaying with a noisy, rushing sound.

**Synthetic** *adjective*
Made by chemical synthesis to imitate a natural product.

**The price of fame** *noun*
The result of being well-known.

**Throw** *verb*
To put something in a place carelessly or hastily.

**Time-honoured** *adjective*
Respected or valued because it has existed for a long time.

**Totally awesome, man**
An expression that means 'really impressive' (informal use).

**Traumatise** *verb*
To shock or distress someone in a way that produces a lasting effect on their mind.

**Trudge** *verb*
To walk slowly and wearily.

**Unearthly** *adjective*
Unnaturally strange and frightening; very awkward or inconvenient.

**Unique** *adjective*
Being the only one of its kind; unlike any other.

## Notes